MW00333879

The Sourcebook of Contemporary Landscape Design

The Sourcebook of Contemporary Landscape Design

Àlex Sánchez Vidiella

COLLINS|DESIGN

An Imprint of HarperCollins*Publishers*

HarperCollins books may be purchased for educational, business, or sales promotional use.
For information, please write: Special Markets Department, HarperCollins*Publishers*,
10 East 53rd Street, New York, NY 10022

First Edition published in 2008 by:
Collins Design
An Imprint of HarperCollins*Publishers*
10 East 53rd Street
New York, NY 10022
Tel.: (212) 207-7000
Fax: (212) 207-7654
collinsdesign@harpercollins.com
www.harpercollins.com

Distributed throughout the world by:
HarperCollins*Publishers*
10 East 53rd Street
New York, NY 10022
Fax: (212) 207-7654

Packaged by:
LOFT Publications
Via Laietana, 32 4.° Of. 92
08003 Barcelona, Spain
Tel.: +34 932 688 088
Fax: +34 932 687 073
loft@loftpublications.com
www.loftpublications.com

Project Coordination & Editor:
Àlex Sánchez Vidiella

Editorial Coordination:
Catherine Collin

Editors:
Montse Borràs, Esther Moreno

Assistant Editor:
Francesc Zamora Mola

Text:
Mar Armengol, Ian Ayers, Francesca Comotti, Sergio Lobato, Álvaro Marcos

Translation:
Antonio Moreno

Art Director:
Mireia Casanovas Soley

Cover Design:
Claudia Martínez Alonso

Layout:
Esperanza Escudero Pino

Library of Congress Control Number: 2008927769

ISBN: 978-0-06-153791-2

Printed in China

First Printing, 2008

Preface	**009**
Introduction	**011**
Big Scale Spaces	**014**
Avalanche Defense Structures in Iceland	018
Aurland Viewpoint	024
Gudbrandsjuvet	032
Sohlbergplassen Viewpoint	040
Pedra Tosca Park	046
Termas Geométricas	054
Termas de Puritama	062
Berestein Cemetery	068
Meerterpen Cemetery	072
Cemetery for the Unknown	078
Bosque de la vida	086
Kiel Triangle Plaza	094
Parque da Juventude	100
Piccadilly Gardens	108
Ourém's Linear Park	114
City Park of Beja	120
La Ereta Park	126
Central Park of Nou Barris and Virrei Amat Square	134
Remodeling of Joan Miró Park	144
Botanical Garden of Bordeaux	154
MFO Park	160
Green Axis 13	166
Landesgartenschau Wernigerode 2006	172
One North Park	182
Sungang Central Plaza	190
Water Landscapes	**200**
Zhongshan Shipyard Park	204
Hai River Embankment Design	210
Remodeling of River Bank	216

Cendon di Silea	222
Welland Canal	232
Dujiangyan Square	236
Pedestrian Bridge	242
HTO	250
Seebad Zweiern	256
Grand Plaza	262
Union Point Park	268
Oriental Bay Enhancement	278
Remodeling of Rauba Capeu	284
Zona de Banys Fòrum	292
Ethnographic Park	304

Urban Spaces — **310**

Traffic Junction Odenskog	314
Diwang Park B	320
Teruel Urban Development	328
Pedestrian Area FUZI	336
Passeig Garcia Fària	344
Fira Montjuïc 2 in Barcelona	354
Clarke Quay Redevelopment	360
Stadtlounge St. Gallen	366
Town Hall Square	374
Bali Memorial	378
Impluvium	386
Harmony of Opposites	392
Trans[plant]	396
In Vitro	402
Litlatún	406
Mente la-menta?	414
Solange	422
Amoeba 2	426

Squares   **432**

Das Águas Square   436

Royal Victoria Square   442

Festplassen   448

Renovation of Čufarjev Square   454

Aristide Briand Square   460

François Mitterrand Square   468

Kreuzlingen Hafenplatz   474

Incontro Tra i Popoli Square   480

Vittorio Veneto Square   486

Square Four Garden   496

Saitama Plaza   504

Manukau Square   508

Enclosed Non-Residential Spaces   **514**

Forest Gallery   518

General Mills Corporate Campus   524

Katharina Sulzer Platz   530

Cour Bleue   540

The Centre for Ideas   544

Residential Spaces   **550**

Las Margas Parks and Gardens   554

Organic Farming Garden   560

Court Square Garden   568

Danse en Ligne   574

Charlotte Garden   580

151 East Jaques Avenue   588

Unterföhring Park Village   594

Directory   **598**

Preface

One aspect of Le Nôtre's genius can be seen in the capacity his works have of offering visitors the perception of a planned universe, free of limits, in an artistic vision of the space. In addition to the prolongation of the Tuileries garden, he designed the axis of the Champs-Elysées to seek a horizon that was, at the time, situated outside the city and relate it to the garden and the palace.

Today, after 350 years of development, this axis offers the whole of Paris and beyond an irreplaceable spatial structure and an unparalleled instrument of cohesion between the quarters and the stages of growth of the city. The axis prolongs the garden along the banks of the Seine within the city and ends at the peak of Chaillot hill, offering a close connection between two points of the initial geography of Paris.

The Tuileries garden on the one side and the horizon of the hill on the other (which has since been magnified, first in the early 19th century by Napoleon's Arc de Triomphe and then in the late 20th century by the Arche de la Défense) engrave the axis in a perfect continuity of the urban spaces on which the city has articulated a fabric over the centuries, making the most of the basis that connects it with the site of the city as a whole. We could say that the city has been developed here on the canvas of a primordial work of art.

This masterly example indicates the extent to which landscape architecture can articulate the scales of a space.

We pass seamlessly from one place to another, not just from one space to the next as if moving between the rooms of a home but, above all, from one place to another which contains or in which something is contained. It is in the scales of these overlapping places that we find our apprehension about the continuity of the world. With their works at all scales, landscape architects are capable of engraving each project within the context of the space that contains it.

These artists work within broad perimeters, for reasons of territorial planning works or to elaborate a landscape atlas, to identify the features that conform the specific nature of a place and the qualities that give it its tone. Because of their ability to analyze perceptions, plus the information they have on natural components and the history of human actions, they can identify the landscape structures that traverse a place and on which a project can be built that draws out its main characters.

Thanks to their understanding of landscape structures and the reasons why a place gives off a specific feel, landscape architects can help mark infrastructures on a territory that would otherwise run the risk of disfiguring it: highways and motorways are high-speed paths they organize in the same way in order to offer users the best possible vision of the territories they cross. Today they have the job of engraving wind parks on the landscape in the best possible conditions of perception. The development of cities and the formation of new neighborhoods are increasingly appealing to landscape architects, who bring to the team of designers (many of whom are also urban developers) an understanding of sites and of the sensitive relations that should be highlighted from among a base of natural elements and the inhabited spaces being developed.

They then organize a subtle continuum of the public space which will lead to the city itself staging the presence of its own geography, first the rivers and banks, and then the woods, hillsides, mountain slopes, horizons and even the rainwater that drains along the sidewalks. They inscribe in the paths of daily activity the visual and sensual perception of nature which the inhabitants of cities are calling out for, making a significant contribution to the implementation of lasting urban development.

Parks and gardens have always held a prominent position within the network of public spaces and are developed as a true urban set-up, articulating natural spaces and paths people can cover on foot or bicycle. The numerous works landscape architects have carried out within the sphere of public spaces speak to the intensity awarded the city by a concept that takes into account an expanded context of territory as well as the consideration of the strata that compose a place, whether natural or historic.

This approach to the landscape, strengthened through the gentle art of gardens and the understanding of natural elements, is able to provide the balance, fluidity and articulation of spaces that enable us to take even greater enjoyment from its qualities and help us feel at one with the world. It is within the heart of a garden that we find this special mission of relating scales, as gardens have from the very start been a reflection of the world, and the landscape architect their artist.

Michel Collin,
Landscape Architect D.P.L.G., Urban Environment Consultant, has designed projects rehabilitating urban gardens such as the Parc de Buttes-Chaumont in Paris. Besides his commitment to a firm, he consults for the State Services at the Département de la Seine Saint Denis.

Introduction

Contemporary landscape architecture is colourful. In the last decade we have witnessed a strong turning towards the use of contrasting colors in the urban setting, as well as in the more rural projects. Powerful and often aggressive forms are dominating the scenes. The trend was originally released in Catalonia (Spain) in the 90s. This introduction of minimalist forms to landscape architecture has widely spread throughout the world since then.

More focus has been set on the need for biological diversity, sustainable design and less resource consumption, thus reflecting the overall social concern worldwide. But the most trendsetting development today is certainly in the urban context. Cities are increasing in size everywhere, and it leaves us with lots of questions and responsibilities for future generations. Therefore the most projects are located in the central areas. A lot of streets and squares are renewed, restored or newly designed to meet the growing demands for a growing population. City parks and waterfronts are rapidly growing in the former backyards of the cities.

We have witnessed the increased use of recycled materials, and the rehabilitation of derelict areas as means of saving energy. At the same time the opportunity to put new forms or materials in contrast to the existing has been an overall design principle. The project Katharina Sulzer Platz, developed by Vetsch Nipkow Partner Landschaftsarchitekten, shows an illuminating example of this new way of using abandoned industrial sites.

Most of all there has been focus on both developing high quality solutions as well as the use of high quality materials that will mature in time. Parallel to the use of more expensive materials, we have seen the use of strong and beautiful colors in low cost tarmac or concrete surfaces, as seen in Passeig Garcia Fària by Ravetllat & Ribas Arquitectes in Barcelona, in Diwang Park B by Urbanus Architecture & Design in Shenzhen, as well as in Green Axis 13 designed by Burger Landschaftsarchitekten in Munich, Germany. One very interesting approach is the Cour bleue, the blue schoolyard designed by NIP Paysage in Montreal. The simple design using a palette of only three colors, shows how subtle the use of colored bitumen really can be, by only adding a drop of white.

Frequently the concepts clearly have an artistic approach. This can only be related to the increased importance of the landscape projects.

The contrast in bringing urban forms and materials into rural settings will provide new dimensions into international landscape design, as seen in the Norwegian viewpoints in Aurland, by Todd Saunders/Saunders Architecture, and Stor-Elvdal, developed by Carl-Viggo Hølmebakk.

And of course, poetic silence is still a main feature in landscaping, which is elegantly visualized in the Cemetery for the Unknown, designed by Hideki Yoshimatsu & Archipro Architects in Hiroshima. Here elegant design combined with low cost materials shows the world how simple and sophisticated noble design really can be.

The re-use of crushed concrete together with river stones and steel rods makes a silent entrance to the afterworld. From the quiet cemetery to busy city life is really a big step, but the quietness we find in the Hiroshima graveyard, can also be felt in the closed garden at the General Mills Corporate Campus, designed by Oslund & Associates in the United States. The design is more abrupt, and there are a lot of elements in contrast, but the impression is whole and it leaves you with a kind of quietness in the end.

But maybe the most artistic and poetic entry is made by the young architects from Girona (RCR Aranda Pigem Vilalta Arquitectes) in their project Pedra Tosca Park using corten steel, rocks and boulders to create a highly refined sunken garden. This is their way of design, it is their way of using simple materials in a structural sense and the sketches for the project are so appealing that you might hang them on the wall in a gallery.

The book also includes a smaller section of four urban plazas. The presumably low cost square in Slovenia (Renovation of Čufarjev Square, Scapelab) shows how one can create a wonderful place for the public with small means. Colored tarmac together with distinct colors and water jets give this square a unique expression in contrast to the surrounding mountains.

The Manukau Square (David Irwin) shows a typical example of modern, aggressive forms; clearly defined lines and areas, bold design, modern materials and contrasting colors. It looks clean and straight forward, linking the adjacent buildings together. The sunken garden Saitama Plaza (PWP Landscape Architecture) is very elegant and the visualization of the changing seasons is a model for everyone. The Norwegian square, Festplassen (Landskap Design) is an interpretation of aggressive, modern forms into an austere, granite symphony with focus on the stone's many different faces; how the stone's expression changes with the changing weather and the surface's different character.

What landscape architecture faces today, is the challenge to create places where people can congregate and enjoy themselves. The Pedestrian Area FUZI (AllesWirdGut Architektur) in Innichen, Italy, clearly demonstrates elegant, minimalist design with the calm, central pool reflecting the sky: a place for contemplation as well as for busy city street life. The gentle use of gray and black clearly accentuates the small items of red, which are used with such refinement.

Extensive use of light in landscapes is a main feature throughout the world. We are paying more attention to low energy light sources than we did in the past, and the new energy-saving LED components are widely used.
Light is used with great care in the new landscape projects, from the close-to-nothing in the austere Zulzer Areal to the Clarke Quay Redevelopment (SMC Alsop) which shows a futuristic Disney-like lighting concept.

Water is maybe the most widely used effect, besides artificial lighting, in new landscaping projects. We find a strong wish in cities by the sea to rehabilitate the shores or inner harbors. Former derelict areas like abandoned wharfs and factories are being transformed into leisure areas for a growing population. The coastline of Barcelona is well-known. Starting with demolition of the Barceloneta area in the late 80s, the waterfront of the Catalonian metropolis is, for the time being, developed all the way north to the latest major projects in the Forum area. The Zona de Banys Fòrum (BB & GG Arquitectes) has become an icon of the city, with the huge solar panel and the bold shape of the terrain. Another example is the HTO (Janet Rosenberg & Associates) public beach in Toronto, where green dunes are planted with willow trees and silver maples. The generous sandy beach is peppered with tall yellow umbrellas, and a wooden boardwalk is literally at the water's edge.

But not every landscape project is situated at ground level. The Montreal Impluvium roof project (NIP Paysage) shows an, up to now, not fully utilized space for landscaping. This vast area on top of the Worlds Cities rooftops, would be a very interesting field for the future. To create biodiversity on top of buildings would indeed be welcomed. This could really mean that we in some way manage to restore the land we occupy.

The Sourcebook of Contemporary Landscape Design is a majestic book which provides you with a worldwide review of landscaping projects. Projects are chosen from all over the world to match this objective.

So, why have these projects been selected? Why are they representatives for the last decade´s development in landscape architecture? In my opinion, they are examples of places you will remember. Places that leave a distinct impression in your memory once you have seen them. Why is that so? I think it has something to do with your references. These are traces of the past, which are left in your memory throughout your existence. These traces are cultural reflections and will differ from continent to continent, from country to country, city to city. But due to today's mobility, your references could easily be from Florence, or from Bejing or Quebec, rather than from your own neighborhood. So, I think the reason why some places make an impression is because they make you feel good. This means that the place does not have to be beautiful, expensive or with an eloquent design, but it has to be nice. Nice is when children are playing and laughing. Nice is when you hear church bells in the silence of a Sunday morning in the autumn. Nice is when you lie on your back in a green field facing the drifting clouds in the sky.

The shaping of land, water and vegetation are the main features of landscape architecture. Adding color and light, you do reflect the modern way of landscaping. This leaves clearly specific impressions and powerful expressions on the viewer. It could be the contrasting, exceptional and colorful concrete sculpture that dominates the site, or it could be the expressive silence from the wind in the trees.

Editor Àlex Sánchez Vidiella has put a lot of effort into making this book a review of the world's most important landscape projects from the last decade. The book contains 82 different projects, divided into six categories: big scale spaces, water landscape, urban spaces, squares, enclosed non-residential spaces and residential spaces. This book, The Sourcebook of Contemporary Landscape Design, will without doubt become a rich and varied Encyclopedia of Landscape Architecture for the first decade of the new millennium.

Arne Sælen

Arne Sæelen is a social scientist who gratuated from the Universities in Bergen (UIB) and Oslo (UIO) in 1976. He also got a degree in landscape architecture at The University of Life Sciences (UMB) in 1997. He was a professor at the Norwegian University of Science and Technology (NTNU) between 1997 and 2007. Since 2004, he has been working as a Professor at The University of Life Sciences (UMB) in Oslo. He has won several awards in international competitions designing landscape projects and he has taken part in different forums and biennals.

Big Scale Spaces

Interventions in Natural Areas

Cemeteries

Urban Parks & Gardens

01 Avalanche Defense Structures in Iceland
Siglufjordhur, Iceland

02 Aurland Viewpoint
Aurland, Norway

03 Gudbrandsjuvet
Gudbrandsjuvet, Norway

04 Sohlbergplassen Viewpoint
Stor-Elvdal, Norway

05 Pedra Tosca Park
Les Preses, Spain

06 Termas Geométricas
Parque Nacional de Villarica, Chile

07 Termas de Puritama
San Pedro de Atacama, Chile

08 Berestein Cemetery
's Graveland, The Netherlands

09 Meerterpen Cemetery
Zwaanshoek, The Netherlands

10 Cemetery for the Unknown
Mirasaka, Japan

11 Bosque de la Vida
Leioa, Spain

12 Kiel Triangle Plaza
St. Louis, MO, USA

13 Parque da Juventude
São Paulo, Brazil

14 Piccadilly Gardens
Manchester, United Kingdom

15 Ourém's Linear Park
Ourém, Portugal

16 City Park of Beja
Beja, Portugal

17 La Ereta Park
Alicante, Spain

18 Central Park of Nou Barris and Virrei Amat Square
Barcelona, Spain

19 Remodeling of Joan Miró Park
Barcelona, Spain

20 Botanical Garden of Bordeaux
Bordeaux, France

21 MFO park
Zürich, Switzerland

22 Green Axis 13
Munich, Germany

23 Landesgartenschau Wernigerode 2006
Wernigerode, Germany

24 One North Park
Singapore, Singapore

25 Sungang Central Plaza
Shenzhen, China

Photo © Omar Ingthorsson, Sigurjon Johsson, Steingrimur Kristinsson, Thrainn Hauksson

Avalanche Defense Structures in Iceland

Siglufjordhur, Iceland   2002

LANDSCAPE ARCHITECTS
Landslag ehf Landslagsarkitektar FÍLA
Client: Icelandic Ministry for the Environment
Town of Siglufjordhur

PARTNERS
Reynir Vilhjalmsson (project manager); VS
Consulting Engineers (pre-design); Hnit Ltd,
VSO Consulting Engineers Ltd (engineers);
Heradsverk Ltd, Sudurverk Ltd (contractors)

AREA
9,687,519 SF

COST
15,000,000 euros

In Iceland, one result of the numerous avalanches that have come to destroy entire villages is that the government has decided to adopt a prevention strategy, such as the planning and construction of barriers and other implementations for reducing the risks involved. Since 1997, Iceland has been busy implementing these defense structures in the areas designated as being most vulnerable. One of these areas, the small seaside town of Siglufjordur, may be found a few miles south of the polar Arctic Circle. Behind this town the mountains climb as high as 3,281 feet, posing a serious risk of avalanche for the town below during the long winter months. A team of technicians and landscapers sought a solution: the answer is more than just a defensive barrier or preventive measure.

The project is based on detailed studies of the environment and its bearings, proposing a transformation of these barriers into something advantageous to the population. The idea is to create a recreational area and, at the same time, soften the often overwhelming image of the mountains. The project consists of a system composed of two parallel earth walls: one at 656 and the other at 2,297 feet long, each with a variable height between 49 and 66 feet, and six walls and dikes that function as containers for the fallen masses of snow.

So that these barriers aren't too overwhelming themselves, their widths vary, giving them a more organic and wavy geometric shape that fits into the landscape. This prevention system provides security and a series of recreational activities during the summer, as well as a few paths for hikers. The end of the barrier, beside the sea shore, is a bulwark that creates a new elevated point from which the surrounding landscape can be admired.

Photomontage

Diagram

Sketch

Site Plan

Photos © Todd Saunders, Michel Perlmutter

Aurland Viewpoint

Aurland, Norway   2005

LANDSCAPE ARCHITECTS
Todd Saunders/Saunders Architecture, Tommie Wilhelmsen/Sivilarkitekt MNAL

CLIENTE
*Norwegian Transport Department
Partners: Node AS (structure); Veidekke AS (contractor); Asplan Viak (consultant)*

AREA
110 F x 13 F x 44 F

COST
2,162,700 euros

Three hours from Bergen, the second most important city in the country, Aurland is a small town situated in one of the largest and most spectacular fjords on Norway's east coast. In 2004, the Norwegian Highway Department (*Statens Vegvesen*) called on three architectural studios to design a scenic lookout over Aurland, where one of Norway's most beautiful views can undoubtedly be had. The chosen project was that of the Canadian, Todd Saunders, and the Norwegian, Tommie Wilhelmsen. It was titled *640 m over Aurland and 20.120 km from Tokyo* and was inaugurated in June of 2006.

First nature, then architecture. Under this fundamental premise did Saunders and Wilhelmsen begin their design. Improving the beauty of the surroundings was impossible. In turn, it is very important not to destroy this area's unique atmosphere and fill it with unnecessary architectural elements. That's why the solution

appeared on its own, based on a type of non-intervention, or, a minimalist conception of the overlook. It wasn't about modification, but the conservation and contemplation of the existing nature. The result is a wooden platform 13 feet wide by 98 feet long, a type of structure in the air, with no closed border. In fact, it has the opposite: only a sheet of glass impedes the visitor from advancing the final 30 feet to the platform's edge. This leaves the lookout open to the countryside and the horizon before the viewer's very eyes and spirit. This way, anyone with the will to climb the 1,969 foot incline to the glass sheet on foot will be greeted with the manifest views of the turquoise fjords, the surrounding mountains and the dense forest of pine trees, all without any visual obstacle. The locale's obsession with purity also called for the removal of the old bus and car parking lot. It's been placed farther away from the platform, at a higher level.

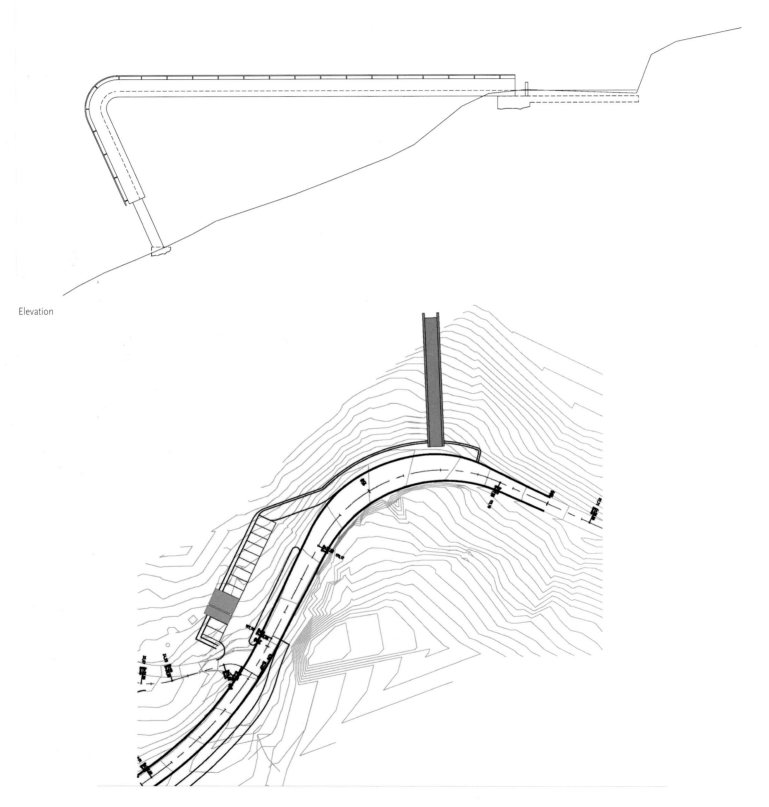

Elevation

Site Plan

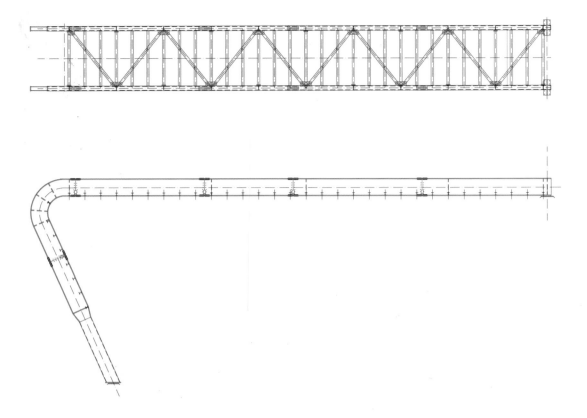

Structural Plan & Elevation

The platform is supported by 30 foot high steel pillars covered with wood at the top, which lends continuity to the platform. With this, a type of ramp was created to accentuate further the idea of jumping off into thin air.

Photo © Jensen & Skodvin Arkitektkontor

Gudbrandsjuvet

Gudbrandsjuvet, Norway   2007

LANDSCAPE ARCHITECTS
Jensen & Skodvin Arkitektkontor

CLIENT
Knut Slinning, Roads Department

PARTNERS
Jan Olav Jensen, Børre Skodvin, Torunn Golberg, Helge Lunder, Torstein Koch (design); Finn Erik Nilsen, Multiconsult AS Year (consultants)

AREA
6,458 SF

Located in the Norwegian region of Nord-dal, along the route that brings tourists from Geiranger Fjord to Trollstigen, Gudbrandsjuvet borders the Reinheimen National Park, known for its spectacular waterfalls. Of modest size, the waterfalls are located in a particularly fascinating landscape, noted for deep rocky ravines that contrast with the green vegetation. The glacial water has shaped the stones and created a unique environment where the water's mist and the waterfall's rumble are melded into the spectacular views.

Visited by hundreds of tourists each year, the landscape of this natural attraction has been the object of replanification. Different interventions by the same team of architects have created a whole, while each maintains a certain independence of expression. A "landscape hotel" situated on an old estate and service areas accompany the most important intervention yet: a panoramic route above the waterfalls created by footbridges and scenic viewing points.

The scenic lookout is built to take advantage of a natural projection in the ground; it's built around the perimeter of this out-jutting and enlarges it with a footbridge that hangs out over thin air. The footbridge's curved and sinuous shape is highlighted by its handrail, composed of parallel metallic tubes. Light, organic and providing only the most delicate impact on the surrounding landscape, the lookout comes to an end after the bridge, on the other side of the river, where it takes on a different set of characteristics. It loses its sinuous character to become a set of straight lines and sharp angles, while the metallic handrail is replaced by cement and glass panels. The entire run is transformed into a stronger and more identifiable architectural gesture.

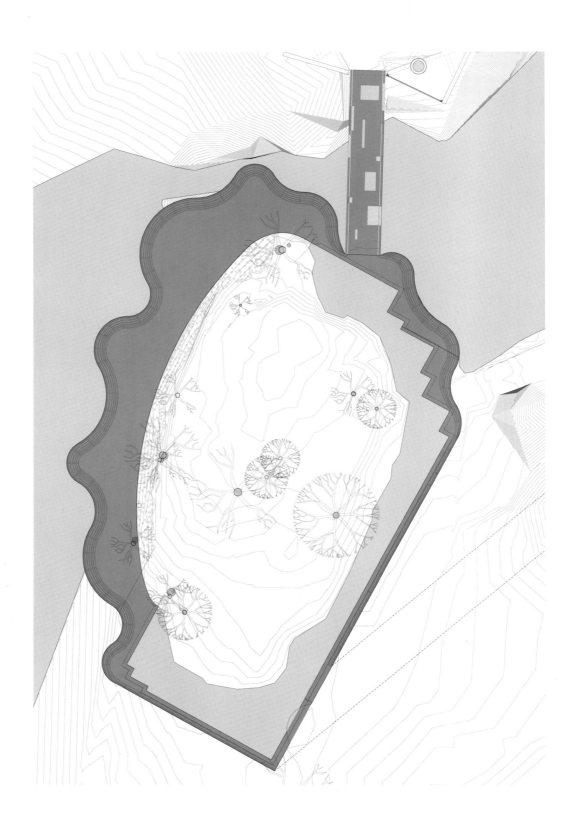

Gudbrandsjuvet is a tourist attraction thanks to its spectacular landscape of waterfalls and ravines. The intervention is located in just the right spot for taking in the best views and forms a path that functions as a scenic lookout for visitors to use.

Platform Plan

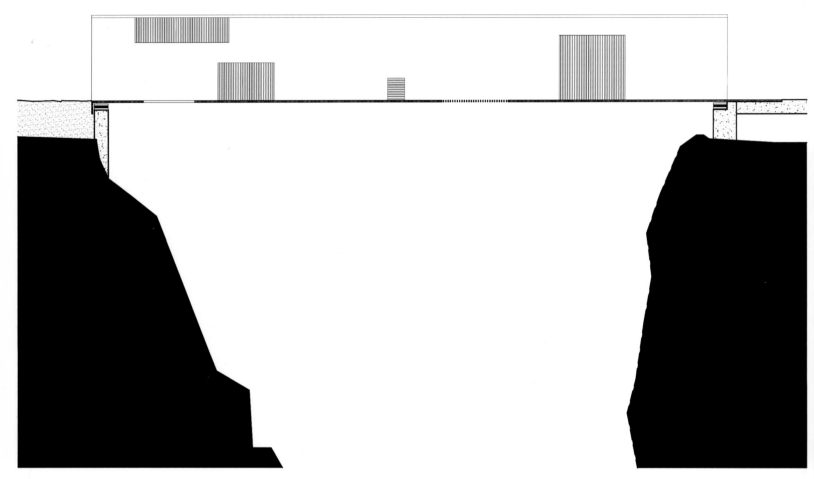

Bridge Section

Platform Section

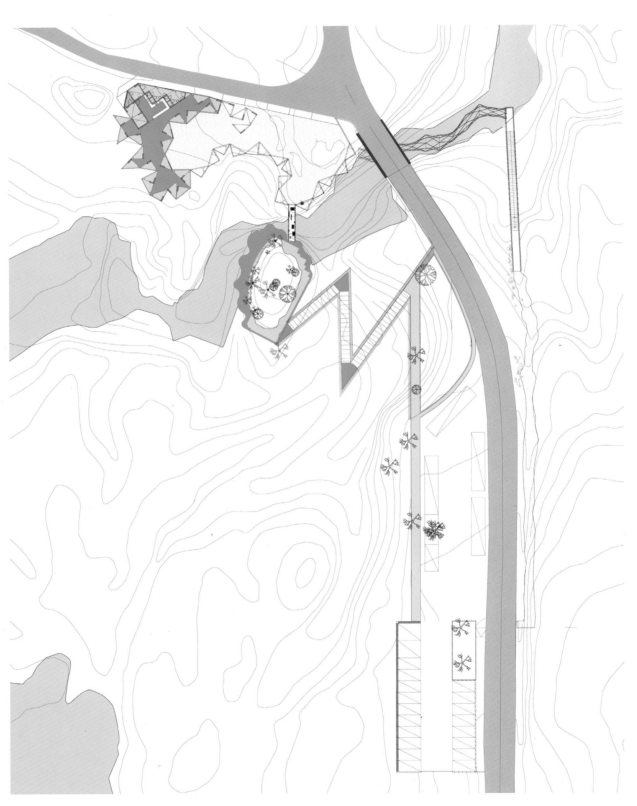

Site Plan

Photo © Carl-Viggo Hølmebakk, Rickard Riesenfeld, Ellen Ane Krog Eggen, Helge Stikbakke

Sohlbergplassen Viewpoint

Stor-Elvdal, Norway   2006

LANDSCAPE ARCHITECTS
Carl-Viggo Hølmebakk

CLIENT
Helge Stikbakke, National Road Department

PARTNERS
Chirsine Petersen (team); Terje Orlien, Kristoffer Apeland (structural engineer)

AREA
82 F (path)

This architectural presence was designed with simplicity and caution to prevent tourists from stomping through the delicate environmental balance of Stor-Elvdal, a locale famous for its enchanting nature and the magnificent views of both lake and mountaintops.

A priority of the project was to find a more effective solution to typical tourist sign-posts like fences, posters and asphalt paths. Built within the pine forest is an elevated platform accessible by two paths. Its shape is the result of a dual investigation: on one side, the study of the relation between the dense pine forest and the mountains in the background determined the design's geometry; on the other side, the topography of the trees was digitized to find the spot with the most scenic viewpoints. These studies prevented both having to cut down trees and having the cement work damage the roots of the trees.

The platform is made of concrete and connected to the ground by a series of steel tubes drilled into the rock; thanks to their thin profile the tubes disappear from the composition to help push the platform's organic shape front and center.

In this way, the platform seems to float a few feet off the ground. The curved concrete beams double as a rail all along the platform except for its front part, where something more transparent was used so as to not interrupt the panorama. To similar effect, the pavement has a slight inclination to give the visitor a sensation of being pushed forward. Within the concrete floor, a handful of rectangular openings, enclosed in glass, let natural light pass through to the terrain below the platform. This prevents the vegetation that grows there from being damaged by this new architectural structure. From the platform, a staircase connects visitors with the surrounding nature and the lake below.

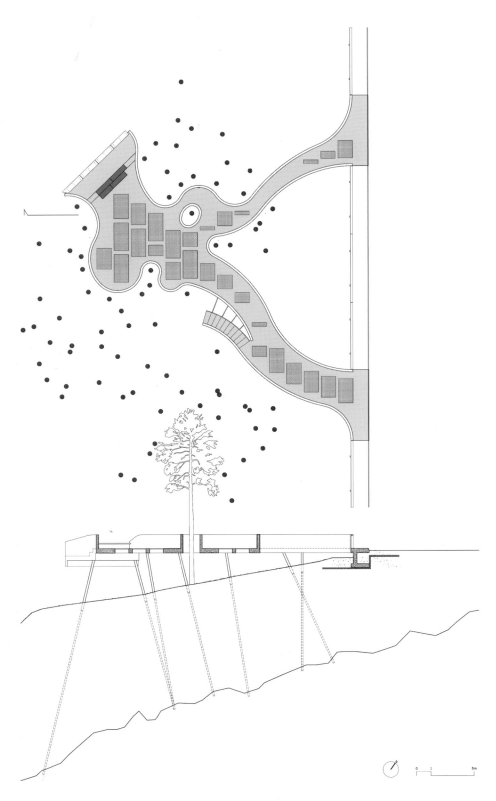

In this design, respect for the surroundings was a priority. The platform's cement structure is connected to the terrain by a series of steel tubes drilled into the rock, some as deep as 39 feet into the ground. This plan avoided excavation that might have damaged the roots of the trees.

Plan & Section

Photo © Eugeni Pons

Pedra Tosca Park

Les Preses, Spain   2004

LANDSCAPE ARCHITECTS
RCR Aranda Pigem Vilalta Arquitectes

CLIENT
Ajuntament de Les Preses

PARTNERS
M. Tàpies, G. Puigvert, Blázquez Guanter Arquitectes, P. Llimona (team); Arico Forest SL, Construccions Metàl·liques Olot SL (constructors)

AREA
618 acres

COST
243,500 euros

Situated in a volcanic area of Garrotxa, in the north of Catalonia, Pedra Tosca Park is a natural space noted for a rocky extension formed by lava that flowed from the Croscat volcano, which erupted almost ten thousand years before Christ. Forested since then by oak trees, the area suffered massive deforestation at the start of the 19th century as a result of the need for wood and coal. Afterwards began the extraction of volcanic rock and the leveling of the land, aimed at converting the profoundly inhospitable ground into cultivated fields. These same stones were used to build walls that delineated the fields, to build cabins and to form burial mounds.

The Catalonian team keeps the natural ecosystem and the historically man-made changes in the landscape in mind with this project. The study of the geology and landscape in Garrotxa, the geography and the strata of human presence provided the inspiration to create a park that would reinvigorate the old fields that were grown in craters to increase the beauty of this unique environment. The roughness of the predominant material is what stands out, and the architects have intervened in a careful and minimalist fashion. The shapes of the terrain, its colors and textures, are highlighted as a result.

The design also seeks to create a surprising effect on the visitor: the narrow paths that cross the mounds of volcanic stone follow a zigzag path that creates a gradual discovery of each and every successive step. The route is traced by two fences that double as containment walls for the stone mounds. These parallel elements are made of treated steel so that, with the passage of time, they will acquire a color and texture in accord with the rocky landscape. The intervention is notable for its delicate treatment, an abstract and timeless relation with the surroundings and the capacity for visibility of the landscape that it has provided; all while maintaining a subtle and respectful relationship with its location.

*The area's unique morphology, characterized by more than forty volcanic
cones, is the natural setting for this intervention. Pedra Tosca Park is
distinguished for being an environment dominated by Wacke rock.*

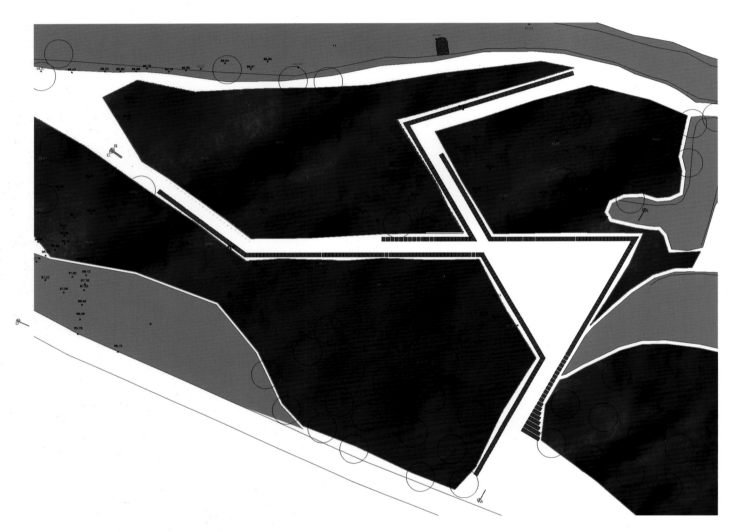

Plan

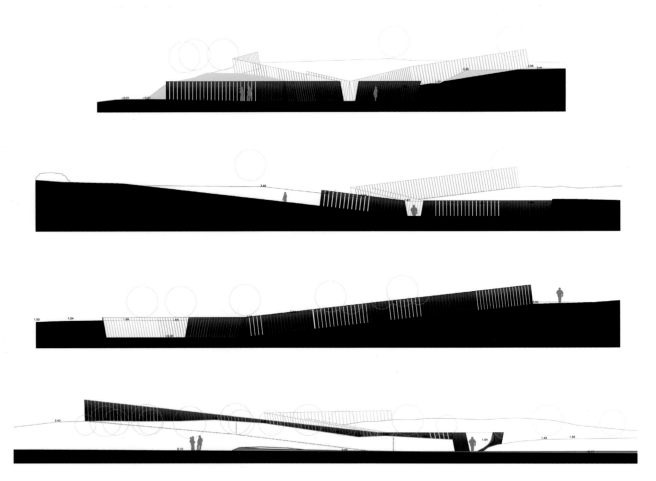

Sections

Conceptual Sketches

Conceptual Sketches

Conceptual Sketches

Photo © Guy Wemborne

Termas Geométricas

Parque Nacional de Villarica, Chile   2004

LANDSCAPE ARCHITECTS
Germán del Sol

CLIENT
Termas Geométricas Ltda

PARTNERS
José Luis Ibáñez, Carlos Venegas (architects)

AREA
1,236 acres

These "geometric hot springs" spout naturally from a third of a mile long ravine in the forests of the Villarica Volcano National park, in the Patagonian region of Chile. They're comprised of over 60 thermal water fountains measuring an average of 176°F. Its orography, particularly inhospitable, is composed of two rocky, extremely steep slopes, at the bottom of which the water flows its course. In a locale that was previously almost inaccessible, the project consisted of the development of some of these fountains to convert them into recreational hot springs.

Water, rocks and dense vegetation provide a natural frame around an intervention that respectfully situates itself within the landscape. Along 1,476 feet of ravine, twenty natural pools are cut from the riverbed's torrent. A wooden footbridge connects them and constitutes the only access to this group of pools. This continuous ramp, without steps, is the route that provides access over the entire ravine to find and choose a more

or less intimate corner from which to enjoy the hot springs. Below its planks, in a wooden canoe, runs the water that keeps the ground's temperature mild even in the winter. Along the footbridge, various terraces are provided for rest when the orography permits; likewise with the cabins provided for changing clothes or sitting around an open fire. The geometry of the area, composed by a succession of straight and precise segments, together with the color red, contrasts with the natural shapes that surround it.

The pools are made of reinforced concrete, built into the rock and dressed with local stone. The footbridges and terraces are made of treated Coihue wood that, along with the support pillars and the rails, have been painted red. The shed is made of the same paved wood and assembled with pillars and trusses, while the deck atop the waterproof planks carries a stratum of cultivated earth and grass.

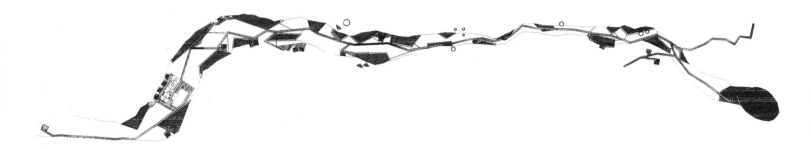

Path Plan

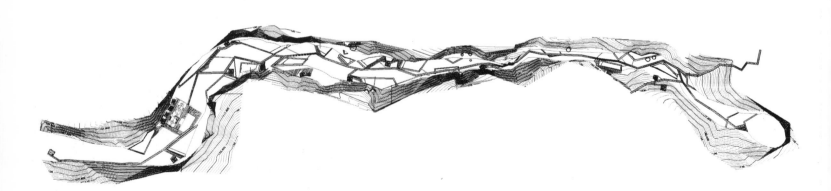

Site Plan

Twenty pools made of reinforced concrete and covered with local stone are carved directly into the rock. The ramp that connects these pools is supported by red pillars of treated wood. The design's will is to highlight the natural over the man-made; this way the beauty of the place is emphasized.

Photo © Guy Wemborne

Termas de Puritama

San Pedro de Atacama, Chile 2000

LANDSCAPE ARCHITECTS
Germán del Sol

CLIENT
Consejo de los Pueblos Atacameños

PARTNERS
Horacio Schmidt, Nicole Labbé, Carlos Venegas, Hernán Fierro (architects and design); Fernando del Sol, Enzo Valladares (structures); Salfa SA (constructor); Rubén Ossandón, Jean Paul Barthou (management); Renato Lorca, Francisco Cervantes (consultants)

AREA
148,263 acres

In a valley hidden 37 miles northeast of the town of San Pedro de Atacama, in the Chilean desert that borders Bolivia, sit the Puritama Hot Springs. These are constantly flowing thermal springs that form natural pools in the middle of a completely arid and inhospitable countryside that for centuries have given the local population a unique source of recreation. The intervention, covering a 148,263 acre country property, was completed by a hotel facility that promised to hand it over to a board of Atacamanian villages, which since then has taken charge of its maintenance and collects its income for the local communities. The cleaning up and improvement project itself was minimal in an attempt to preserve the original natural landscape.

The river runs along a 9 mile long ravine and of its many natural wells, barely more than one has been the object of intervention. This was subjected to almost invisible strokes that hardly affected the territory: the wells

were made larger to provide for more comfortable bathing in the hot waters, while a wooden footbridge spans the channel, mixing in with the vegetation that surrounds it. This dock carries visitors to the pools and invites them to stroll along the river at a height slightly above ground level to avoid any damage to this exceptional locale's delicate ecosystem. The footbridges are made of treated wood and tinted red without covering the grain. The treatment is to protect the wood from the ultraviolet rays that are particularly damaging in Atacama.

The color red, obviously foreign to the valley's natural landscape where the sun can be so intense as to make chromatic differences imperceptible, comes from the Atacamanian culture. A sign of stable human presence, red is the color used to paint the caves and symbolizes life. Another part of the whole is the two small reinforced concrete structures, covered in white plaster, that house all of this establishment's necessities.

The Puritama Hot Springs cover over a half a mile of riverbed, creating many natural wells that have been used since the beginning of time by the local population. The pools and the footbridge attempt to enhance the locale's uniqueness and permit, at the same time, the sustainable use of these hot springs.

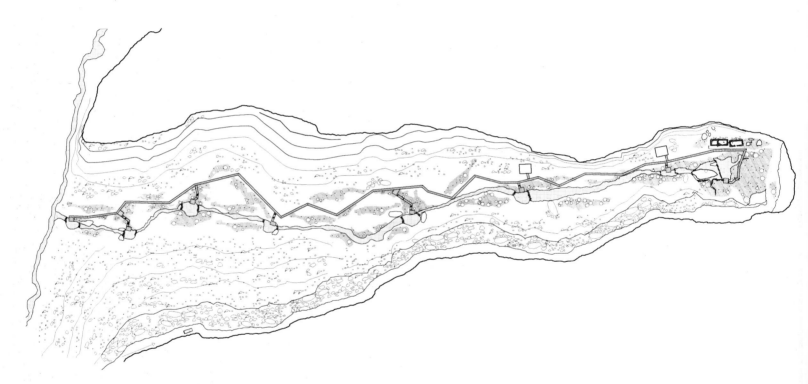

Site Plan

Photo © Karres en Brands Landschapsarchitecten, Chiel van Diest

Berestein Cemetery

's Graveland, The Netherlands   2000

LANDSCAPE ARCHITECTS
Karres en Brands Landschapsarchitecten

CLIENT
Municipality of 's-Graveland

PARTNERS
*Sylvia Karres, Bart Brands, Marie-Laure
Houdemakers, Rudolf Zielinski (project
architects); Grontmij BV (construction
manager)*

AREA
107,639 SF

COST
900,000 euros

The Berestein cemetery, in the north of Holland, is located in an area that already in the 17th century was cultivated in accordance with the landscape. It's a unique setting, with twenty-seven similar fields holding a preponderancy of parks and gardens. This locale has been modified over the years without losing its beauty and its important ecological and environmental value. The project oversees the enlargement of an old cemetery surrounded by a forest of oak, acacia and birch trees.

In the central area, a double row of lime trees at the entrance serves as an axis beside which opens an area of pathways and gravestones. On the side opposite the entrance, the path leads to a large prairie cultivated with cherry trees. The old cemetery is presented as an open-air room and the new intervention aimed to accentuate this characteristic. The enlargement colonizes the empty spaces of the back field to shape an island surrounded by water and connected to the existing cemetery by a main axis that separates the island into two symmetrical shapes. The space inside this oval is planted on a grid that holds the graves, the cherry and 20 foot tall lime trees. On a lower level, 3 foot tall beech bushes are also arranged in grid form.

In a densely-treed transition area between the new and old cemeteries, the chapel can be found as if it were a hidden treasure. Rectangular and sporting a curved roof, it is built so as to seem as if it's not touching the ground. The two transparent walls bring the ferns closer while the connection with the rest of the cemetery is made through a narrow path perpendicular to the main path and notable for its funerary urns, arranged in columns.

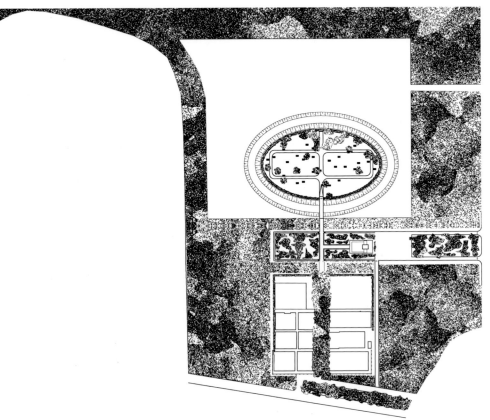

Site Plan

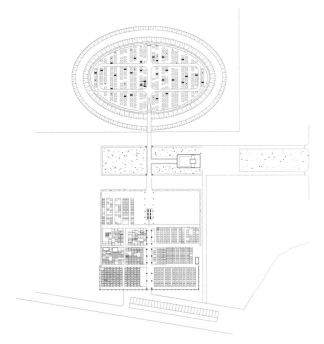

Plan

Photo © Jos van de Lindeloof, Ruud van Zwet

Meerterpen Cemetery

Zwaanshoek, The Netherlands   2002

LANDSCAPE ARCHITECTS
*Jos van de Lindeloof Tuin en
Landschapsarchitectenbureau*

CLIENT
Municipality of Haarlemmermeer

PARTNERS
*Arcadis (plan development); WVAU Architecten
(renovation); Krinkels BV (realization)*

AREA
11.5 acres

COST
1,400,000 euros

The Meerterpen cemetery occupies twenty-nine of the one thousand one hundred and twelve acres assigned to this project and is part of a strategic municipal plan to promote green areas in the eastern part of Harlemmermeer. Amongst the demands the initiative had to satisfy was the implementation in phases of a complete integration with the surrounding environment and adjacent recreational areas and another need that encompassed paying close attention to the needs of a multicultural community. The project presented by the studio of Jos van de Lindeloof encompassed these demands through a symbolic and functional design.
The cemetery makes use of the area's polder to recreate the foliated silhouette of an oak leaf, commonly associated with longevity and eternity. A long path becomes a nerve center that branches out into secondary paths, through a series of bridges, to grant access to the eleven slightly elevated areas for graves. These permit a variety of burial rites. There are fields for spreading ashes, another area for children's graves and an area for crypts. Function determines the height of the tombs: one level for Islamic sepulchers, two levels for private ones and three levels for rentals. A different type of tree has been planted in each area and the space is distributed to favor intimacy, with tree-covered circular terminals that hold chairs designed by Maris van der Made to replace benches and offer views of the lake. Installed in the center of the property is an exact copy of the halls Gerrit Rietveld designed for Wilgenhof cemetery.
The cemetery adapts to the sinuous contours of the lake and the ecological diversity is preserved by combining dry and humid areas. The borders have been forested with an eye towards reinforcing privacy within the space while preventing the surrounding neighborhood from experiencing daily confrontations with death. At the end of the main path is a sculpture by artist Roel Teeuwen. The patterns in the pavement that depict leaves from the trees that flank the path are the work of Eric Odinot.

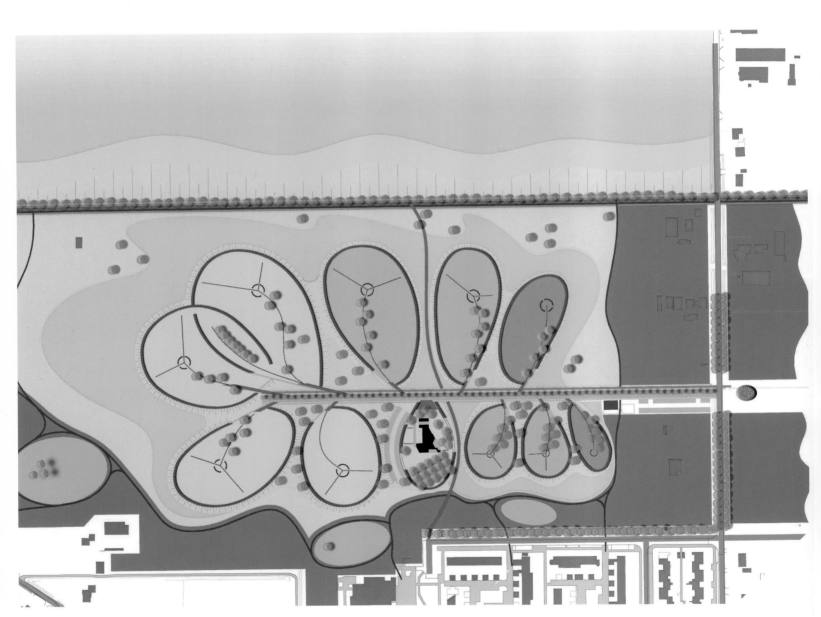

Plan

Photo © Hideyuki Ashiba, Masanori Kato, Earthworks Project, Archipro Architects

Cemetery for the Unknown

Mirasaka, Japan   2004

LANDSCAPE ARCHITECTS
Hideki Yoshimatsu & Archipro Architects

CLIENT
City of Mirasaka

PARTNERS
Hideki Yoshimatsu, Michio Maeda (project architects); Kato-gumi (general contractor)

AREA
3,122 SF

When the decision was made to construct a new dike in the area northeast of Hiroshima's Coast Guard, which entailed the flooding of a large expanse of fields, the local government of the city of Mirasaka urged a specific plan for the affected terrain to reduce the impact of such a huge transformation. One of the resulting projects was this Cemetery for the Unknown, a commemorative space for another cemetery that was submerged under the water's rising tide.

The local population solicited a memorial monument for the nameless tombs that disappeared after the dike's construction; the petition strongly underlined the secular nature of such a monument, completely devoid of any religious symbolatry. The landscaper's solution was to install fifteen hundred six-and-a-half-foot-high stainless steel bars and replant a sacred tree, the *tarayoh*, at the composition's apex. The south side of

the terrain borders another cemetery, from which it has taken its geometric idea of using parallel strips that diagonally cross the terrain. Paths wind throughout this forest of steel bars that, being finely cut, sway slightly with the wind. The dense forest of bars, which stands out against the green vegetation, is anchored to platforms of reinforced concrete covered in river stones. Beside these, other smaller gray stones delineate the path. In the front part of the area, corresponding to the monument's entrance, or, more specifically, off to the sides of the slightly inclined path, these same river stones are flattened beneath subtle metallic frames. The new cemetery offers itself to visitors as a place of intense emotional impact: mysterious and moving in its simplicity, built with complete respect for Japanese tradition.

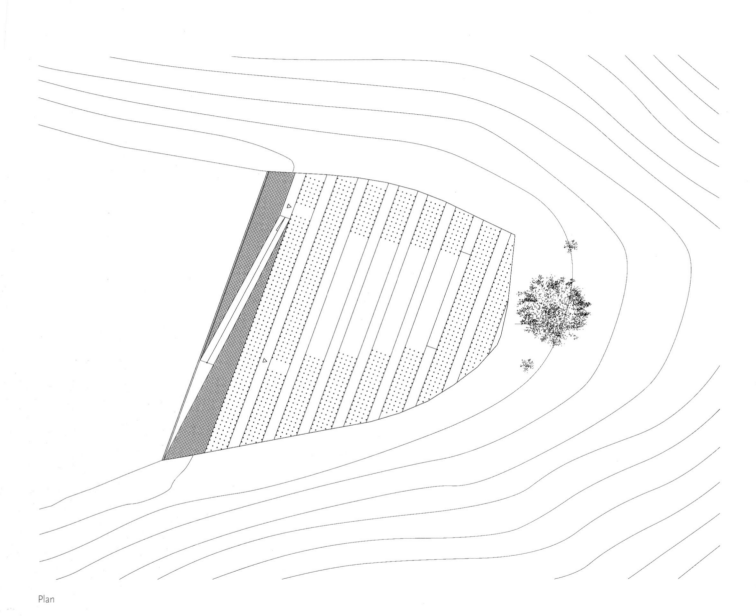

Plan

Sketches

The project was commissioned by the local Mirasaka government to answer the community's need to create a commemorative space for the Cemetery for the Unknown, submerged after the Haizuka dike's construction. The locale holds great emotional and spiritual meaning, emphasized by its minimalist design.

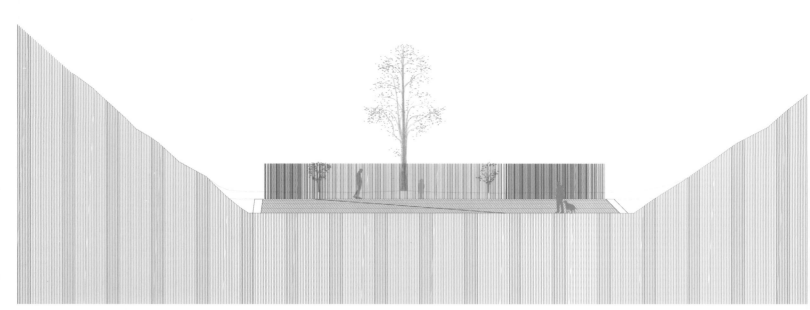

Elevation

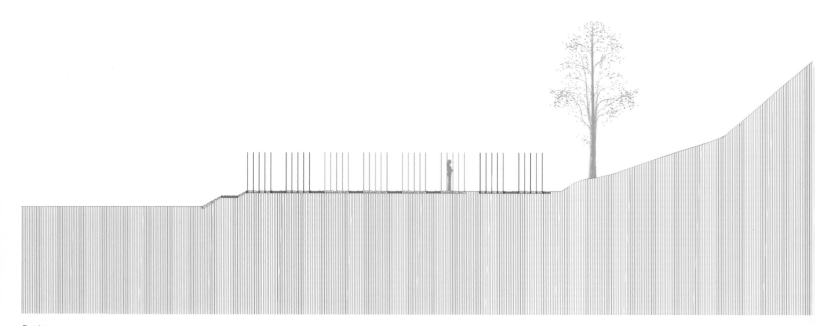

Section

Photo © Mari Carmen Vilà

Bosque de la vida

Leioa, Spain   2003

LANDSCAPE ARCHITECTS
Zade & Vilà Associats

CLIENT
Campus de Leioa, Universidad del País Vasco

PARTNERS
Germán Zambrana-Delgado, Mari Carmen Vilà i Espino (authors); Consultors Tècnics d'Engenyeria i Arquitectura SL, Joan Carles Adell, Francesc Ventura (structure); Rosana Castañón, Sanna Lampainen (3D modeling); Caldesa SA, Francisco Delgado (manufacture)

AREA
5 acres (park)

Some Spanish universities have built monuments to those who've donated their bodies for study and teaching of anatomy. One of these is the University of the Basque Country. The winning effort in the contest held by this same institution offers a uniquely different perspective. A space open to the senses physically, visually and conceptually, devoid of roofs, paths, doors, order, numbers and limits; thus bringing the place closer to the idea of a forest. Here the word forest is understood as a space for change, comprised of mutational material where any element, whether it is people or floral offerings, is a sum of the whole. This idea is developed through a group of sculptures called "The Forest of Life," that distances itself completely from any implication with the concept of cemetery or park.

Located in natural surroundings beside the Cantabrian Sea, the forest is a final resting place for ashes. The project is comprised of twenty trees that hold three hundred twenty urns. Each tree is composed of three parts: a tree well, the trunk and the treetop. The tree well, made of corten steel, is engraved with a number and holds a lighting apparatus. The trunk is the most visible part, with heights that vary between 46 and 59 feet tall, and varied angular turning points that help to make each tree different. Each of the trees is composed of a tube with an 18 inch diameter and united to two metal plates that rotate in a counter-clockwise direction around the tube and confer the whole with dynamism. The funerary urn is located behind a door within the tree. Lastly, the treetop is composed of stainless steel cables 2 centimeters thick and suspended by a stanchion rope system that manipulates the wind so that it makes a resonant sound. The lateral bench is made of iroko wood and contains, in one of its backrests, a place for all of the names of the forest's inhabitants.

The forest, aside from holding the urns within its tubular trunks, also offers itself as a sonorous memory, thanks to the treetops with their linked steel cables that resonate with the wind.

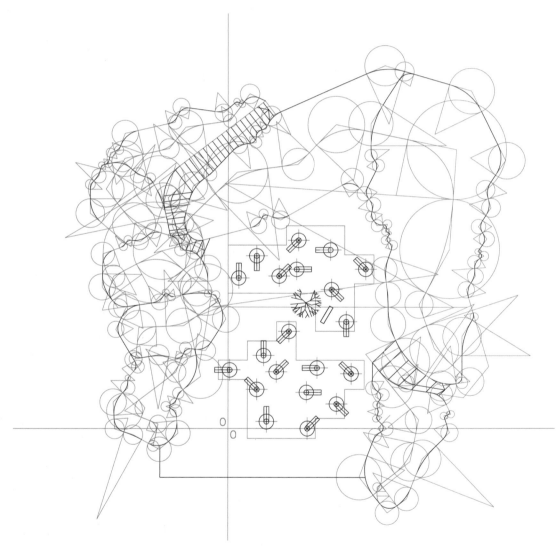

Site Plan

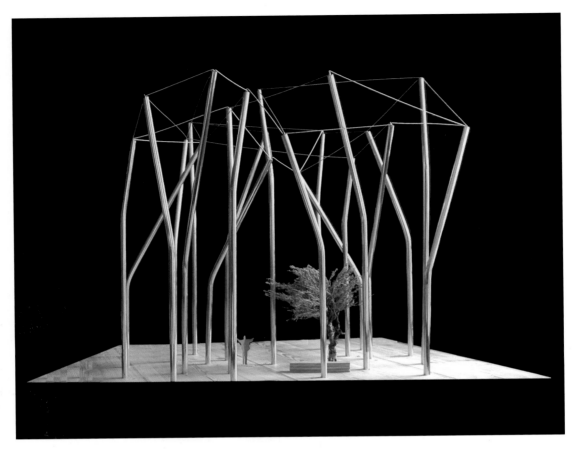

"Forest" Model

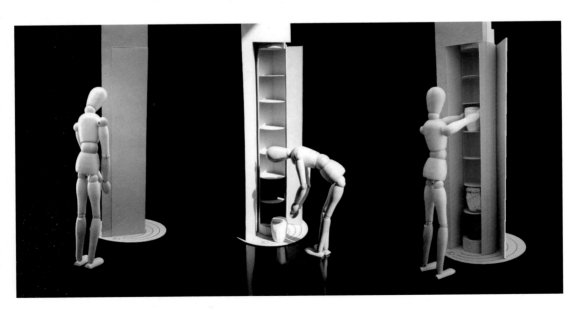

Funerary Urn Models

The wooden bench is an all-purpose seat, comprised of three parts of variable size. Made of treated iroko wood and stainless steel fittings, the bench was planned in such a way as to facilitate its assembly.

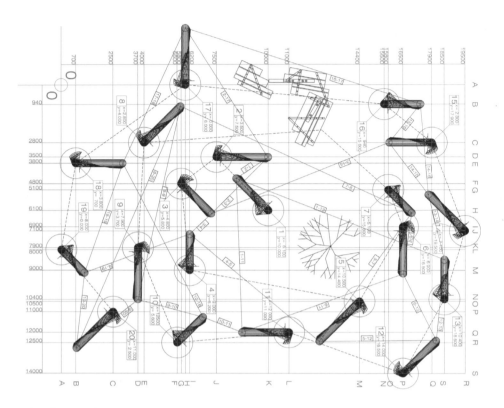

Three-dimensional Representation

Elevation

Photo © PWP Landscape Architecture

Kiel Triangle Plaza

St. Louis, MO, USA   2002

LANDSCAPE ARCHITECTS
PWP Landscape Architecture

CLIENT
Gateway Foundation

PARTNERS
Booker Engineers Architects (civil engineer); R. J. Van Seeters Co Ltd (water feature MEP)

AREA
1 acre

Kiel Triangle Plaza is the result of collaboration between St. Louis state development agencies and the non-governmental Gateway Foundation, which in recent years has contributed to diverse projects for the revitalization of urban landscapes. It's a public space that, located in the center of the city, supplies a plaza with a sports and concert complex, which until this moment had been lacking an exterior space, and connects it with the entrance to a nearby MetroLink station.

The promenade from the plaza to the station, located atop a small hill, is characterized by its accented lighting. The light emanates from spotlights fitted into the rows of stone benches that lead, on the one side, to the pedestrian path, and on the opposite side to a small forest of cypress trees. The promenade ends at the plaza in a semi-circular shape that also grants access

to the arena, thanks to an arc of ten hollow stainless steel panels that radiate light, fog and steam to animate the plaza with spectacu-lar results. The atmosphere creates some shocking effects, lending the location a stage design that is unique in this city. The "walls of fog," 46 feet wide by 46 feet long and just over an inch thick, are presented as a glossy steel frame, covered by thirty-six stainless steel sheets with fog-spewing perforations. At the same time, each panel contains a fluorescent light structure that may be programmed to emit yellow, blue, red as well as secondary colors. This flexibility makes determined effects possible for events and special festivals that, for example, take place in the nearby arena. Also, the circular fountain in front of the panels emits vapors and helps to create a spectacular and magical setting of both light and mystery.

Kiel Triangle Plaza is a small passageway that leads to an office area and an events arena. The plaza is connected to the new MetroLink station. The project is notable for a play of colored light and water evaporated to create special effects.

Plan

Elevation

Photo © Nelson Kon

Parque da Juventude

São Paulo, Brazil   2005

LANDSCAPE ARCHITECTS
Rosa Grena Kliass Arquitetura Paisagística Planejamento e Projetos Ltda

CLIENT
Secretaria da Juventude, Esporte e Lazer do Estado de São Paulo

PARTNERS
José Luiz Brenna (co-author); Alessandra Gizella Silva, Fabiana Frasseto, Gláucia Dias Pinheiro, Mauren Lopes de Oliveira

AREA
2,583,339 SF

Open to the public in 2004, this park located in the north part of the city of Sao Paulo is the result of readapting a space once occupied by a penitentiary. The project, which won a contest in 1999, covers an area of 2,583,360 square feet where prisoner wings have been converted into didactic halls, cultural spaces and health centers, while the outside area has been transformed into a public park.

The green area is divided into three parts that correspond to the three phases of construction: the Sports Park, the Central Park and the Institutional Park. The first was built on a partially abandoned plot of land that was occupied by the penitentiary hospital. Its 376,740 square-foot area gathers sports-related equipment and is structured along an avenue lined with tall trees. This route serves as an important connecting element for the entire park, since it crosses the three areas and is flanked by rest areas with dense foliage and children's recreational equipment.

The Central Park represents the project's green heart. Its 968,760 square feet are covered with large expanses of trees and open meadows. In this space, abandoned structures belonged to the house of detention complex, which was never completely finished, and offers up beams, columns and slabs of stone to be spontaneously covered in vegetation. The metallic and concrete framework is enveloped in a thick tipuana forest that opens to the public by way of a scaffold system of footbridges and allows one to discover new perspectives. A network of secondary paths connects the Central Park with the Institutional Park. This last area serves as a nexus with the city: it's characterized by four penitentiary buildings that have been readapted for public use, a new theater and a large urban square that serves to welcome and direct users towards the various activities the park has to offer.

In the central area we find an enclosure wall and building structures that
are remains of houses that were never completed. They've made use of
these remains by creating a series of footbridges connecting the enclosure
wall with the beams and metal or reinforced concrete columns.

Site Plan

Stairs Section

General Sections

Pavilion Section

Photo © Dixi Carrillo

Piccadilly Gardens

Manchester, United Kingdom   2002

LANDSCAPE ARCHITECTS
EDAW

CLIENT
Manchester City Council

PARTNERS
Barry Jessop (construction manager); Balfour Beatty Civil Engineering Ltd (construction company); Manchester Operational Services (maintenance agent)

AREA
13,5 acres

COST
19,035,000 euros

Manchester is an industrial and crowded city with a cultural scene that is proverbially restless and continually successful. Nevertheless, its urban center is also noted for its lack of ample green spaces. EDAW's project was undertaken in centrally situated Piccadilly Gardens and is the first decisive step in rectifying this situation and regenerating the adjacent areas while they're at it. The space occupied by the park is one of the city's central hubs of communication and transportation: it's surrounded by the bus station, streetcar rails (called metrolink), various taxi stands and a diverse amount of services adjacent to the business area. Traditionally, the gardens were one of the more depressed locales in the area, adorned with rows of bushes and flowerbeds. Its layout and insufficient lighting left it regarded as an unsafe place for the city's inhabitants.

It was declared that these 13.5 centrally-located acres were underutilized, and so the plan of intervention was framed around a desire to create an open and public space of international character. The first process was the remodeling and ground-leveling of the avenues of circulation and the pedestrian walkways within the park and its surroundings. The gardens were redesigned to become a huge grass area divided by two routes and a footbridge, running north to south, which crossed the main fountain's pond. The fountain, devised by Meter Fink, constitutes the heart of the design and is its most dynamic element: a granite ellipse that projects foamy jets of water. These jets interact with the studied lighting scheme that lights up the park at night. The esplanade provides the city with a vast civic space, adequate for holding large scale happenings, like those associated with the 2002 Commonwealth Games. At the south end of the square, the curved pavilion by Tadeo Ando holds a cafeteria and an information office. The construction serves as a physical barrier between the park's uncluttered space and the busy routes for the bus and the metrolink.

The Piccadilly Gardens rehabilitation is the first step in a regeneration of the urban center that rectifies an absence of large green spaces in the city. The park also revitalizes a part in the middle that was affected by an IRA bombing. The most dynamic element is the fountain, situated at the garden's center. Made of granite, it shoots out recreational jets of water.

Site Plan

Perspective

Photo © FG & SC

Ourém's Linear Park

Ourém, Portugal   2005

LANDSCAPE ARCHITECTS
Proap

CLIENT
Cidade de Ourém

PARTNERS
António Garcia Arquitectos (architect); Nuno Jacinto, Mafalda Silva, Sílvia Basílio, António Magalhães de Carvalho (collaborators); João Cristo/Projectual Lda, António Almeida, Ivo Carvalho (consultants); Constructora do Lena, Socoliro, Aquino Rodrigues (contractors)

AREA
968,752 SF

COST
5,000,000 euros

The creation of this space, located in Ribeira de Seiça, corresponds to a hybrid project of urban and environmental renovation aimed at a harmonious and useful coordination between the urban fabric of the area and the beautiful natural surroundings of the river-bank around it. The ensemble covers two important buildings, the Congress building and a municipal market, and is laid out as a navigable and open linear space: pedestrian walkways and a bicycle lane made of porous cement connect the different areas for leisure, games and all types of sports, while bordering the lake and canal system. Market supply is insured by a paved transition area that allows for easy access to the premises. The selection of simple and strong materials reinforces the aesthetic goal of smoothing the transition between the city and its natural surroundings. In the areas for parking and moving traffic, the floors combine gravel with grass and the aforementioned porous cement, which facilitates drainage of rain water into the river.

The layout was designed with the environment's water system in mind while trying to rehabilitate the riverside's metabolism; not only was previous vegetation preserved, but new diverse species of grass, shrubbery and trees were planted while also building four cement docks to prevent the strangulation of the water's natural flow. The right margin, specifically, was reforested with native species and strengthened by the construction of a rocky base that also serves as a border to highlight and protect the dense woodland. The studied alternation of forested areas and clear green esplanades optimizes the architectural functionality and legibility of a natural space that remains urban as well. Powerful bonds are created between the water, land and sky through the skillful combination of nature, technology and urban planning.

The park occupies a navigable and linear surface, totaling 968,752 square feet, which guards the river while adapting to its course of flow and nature. The project offers city inhabitants a contextualized and well-equipped natural space with areas for recreation and sports, including bicycling and skating.

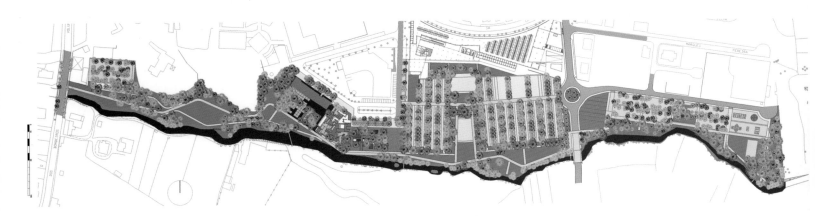

Site Plan

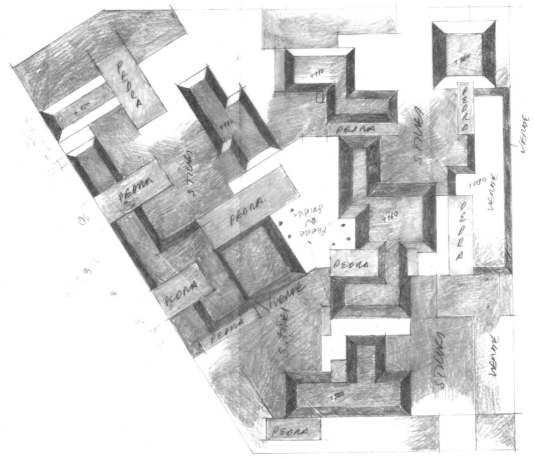

Sketch

Section

Photo © João de Castro

City Park of Beja

Beja, Portugal   2004

LANDSCAPE ARCHITECTS
Arpas Arquitectos Paisagistas Associados,
Santa-Rita Arquitectos

CLIENT
Bejapolis

PARTNERS
Luis Cabral, Lucile Dubroca, Adelaide Sousa
(landscape team); João Santa Rita, Rui Sá
(architect team); Artur Pinto Martins
(structure); HCI, Rozado e Frazão
(constructors)

AREA
17 acres

As with many other cities in the south of Portugal, the city of Beja was delineated behind the old walls that surrounded the hill on which the city was built. Outside the city stretched fertile agricultural plains that, with the urban growth of recent decades, became integrated into the city to create a new crown of homes and equipment. In 2002, it was decided to build the city's park in this area. Beja, at that time, had a vast 17 acre shepard's prairie right at the city's entrance. North of this prairie was the cemetery, on the east, blocks of new homes; the south held an ecologically valuable eucalyptus forest. The new park aspired to create a space for the improvement of the area's environmental condition. It also needed to provide the equipment necessary for a public recreational area—things like bicycling, ball playing, reading below a tree or simply going for a walk around the lake or contemplating the area's rich vegetation.

Nevertheless, this oasis still needed to improve the environmental conditions and to that effect, not only were new native plants grown, but an artificial lake was created to insure the park's irrigation during dry seasons and, at the same time, lend the location a symbolic nature. For this reason, the park also represents a pedagogical labor of approximation with the environment and demonstrates that, despite the limits that nature imposes, man can, with respect and ecological awareness, dominate and perhaps even better a territory.

Architecturally, a highlight is the restaurant building, a modern construction that not only integrates perfectly with the park's landscape but also becomes a fundamental element in the location's accessibility, marking the border between areas for moving traffic and the parking lot. The cement structure dominates the central area beside the lake. These two are integrated by way of footbridges and terraces that invite rest and contemplation of the scenic views offered there. Into one of these terraces has been integrated the support for a waterfall. All this provokes a type of geometric topography where the natural elements synthesize with the architectural elements to create a hierarchy of density and space that modifies as the visitor enters the center of the park, dominated by the restaurant and the lake.

Beja Park unites the old city with one of the new neighborhoods on its periphery. Over the lake, we find footbridges with canopies that protect againt the sun and invite one to relax. The project was born of the necessity to create a space to improve the area's environmental condition and insure the necessary equipment for the public's entertainment and recreation.

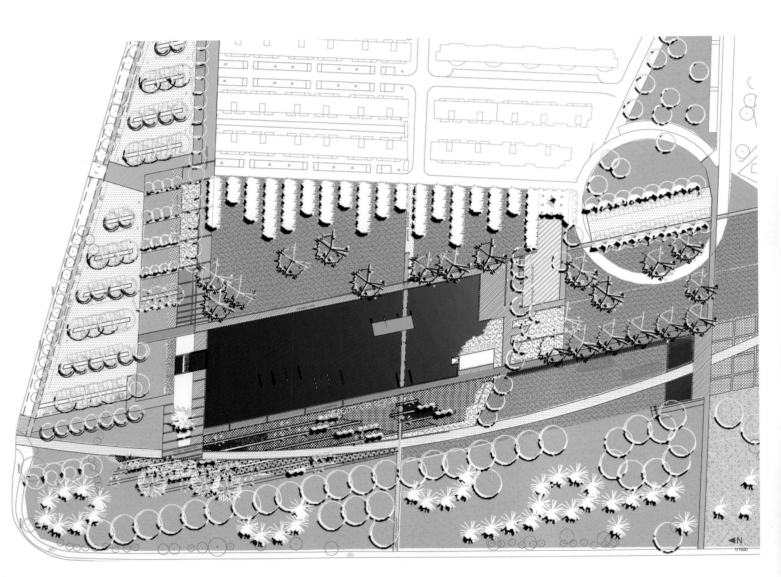

Plan

Sketch

Night Simulation

Photo © Obras Architectes

La Ereta Park

Alicante, Spain   2004

LANDSCAPE ARCHITECTS
Obras Architectes

CLIENT
City of Alicante, Generalitat Valenciana, Patronato Municipal de la Vivienda de Alicante

PARTNERS
Marc Bigarnet, Frédéric Bonnet (project managers); Miguel Salvador Landmann (construction supervision); David Chambole, CYPE SA (consulting structural engineers); Luis de Diego Fort (quantity surveyor); M.ffi Dolores Lozano Sánchez (agronomy engineer)

AREA
755,939 SF

COST
11,869,300 euros

In Alicante, Mt. Benacantil dominates the old historical center, port and sea. Since the time of the Moors, this city icon has housed impressive city wall fortifications and, later on, some vernacular architecture buildings. By constructing this park they've recovered an abandoned geographical landmark that was wasting away. Its steep slope, landslides, southeast orientation and difficult access all contributed to its slow degradation. The intervention plan that resulted from the Europan 3 contest, aimed to reconquer the land and integrate it with the city by restrengthening its ties with the higher parts of the old city center, urban nucleus and port. The intention was to revitalize the mountain and reestablish its natural union with the castle. The landscape architects had three strategies for this intervention: a progression as one went up the hill from more urban to more wild; to take advantage of the technical requirements; and to offer an accessible area joining different territorial

and architectural scales. The park's character changes as one gets further away from the lower area in proximity to the historical center. Visitors who go up towards the castle pass through different areas characterized by more domestic vegetation on the lower part of the hill and wilder vegetation at the top: olive and pine trees make way for the local holm oaks and graminaous plants.

Solutions for technical problems are fundamental in these kinds of areas. Its containment walls, irrigation canals for runoff and drainage systems are all closely connected with the elements composing the park. The terrain first becomes a containment wall and later a façade: the boundary is a path that borders the lower part, and at the same time, assures that rain water is collected; olive trees stabilize the ground and reduce erosion. The transitions between urban architecture, landscaping, and technical scales disappear to form a union with the natural landscape.

With seventeen acres, the park has different areas that range from the most intimate to the most collective, from the most wild and savage to the most developed, from the most limited to the most open. The changing vegetation accompanies visitors on their path to the mountain's summit.

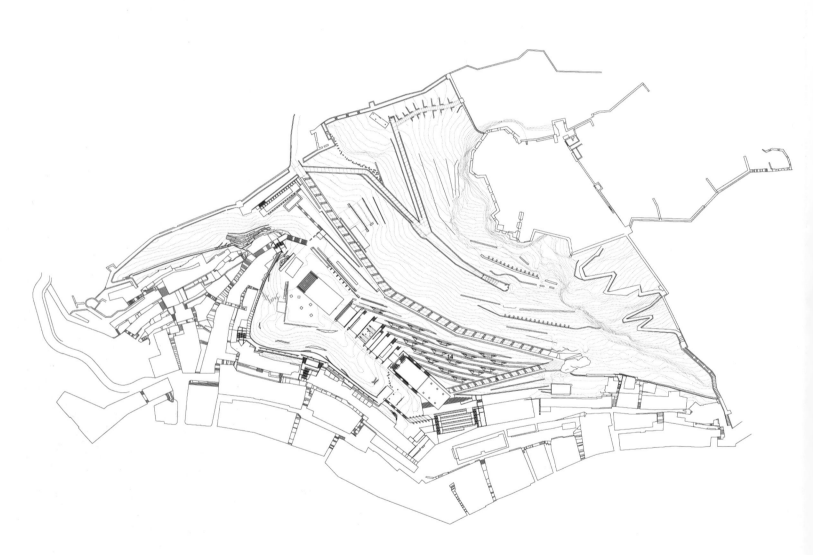

Plan

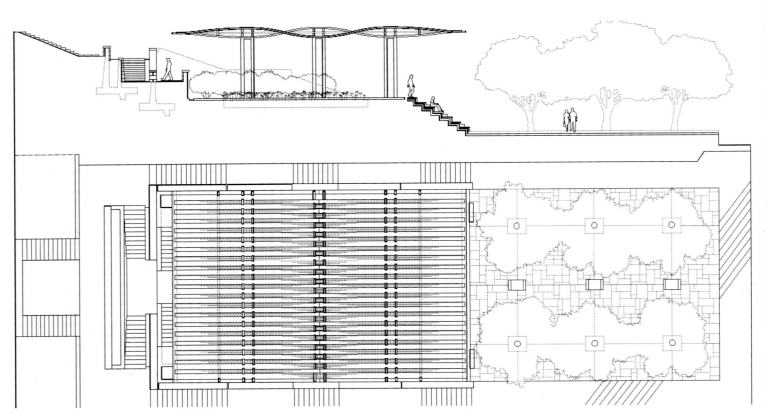

Pavilion Plan & Section

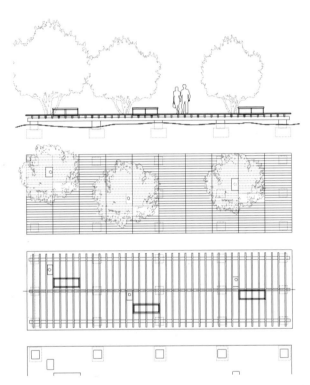

Shelter Plans & Sections

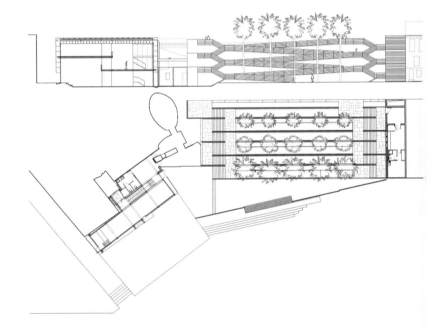

Photo © Sergio Belinchón, Beat Marugg, Arriola & Fiol

Central Park of Nou Barris and Virrei Amat Square

Barcelona, Spain   2007

LANDSCAPE ARCHITECTS
Arriola & Fiol Arquitectes

CLIENT
Pro Nou Barris SA, Ajuntament de Barcelona

PARTNERS
Agustí Obiol (structural engineering); CEA, DB, J. M. Salvany (M&E engineering); Ll. Roig, Ll. Fontanet (technical architects); Ibering Engineering (consultant); Ferrovial, ACS, CESPA, NEXO (general contractors)

AREA
41 acres (park); 182,986 SF (square)

COST
18,187,600 euros

After the 1992 Olympic Games, Barcelona benefited from huge improvements in its urban infrastructure. Without a doubt, one of the most important was the construction of a peripheral ring that improved access to the city from both the Baix and Dalt ring roads. The districts near the ring roads also benefited from these improvements, as in the case of the 3 square mile district of Nou Barris, located in the northeast part of the city and shaped with truly diverse neighborhoods. The renovation plans for this district were very well received by its neighbors, who watched the construction of this huge central park. This became the principal intervention in the northeast part of Barcelona.

The project was designed and carried out by Arriol & Fiol Architects and the principal objective was to create a green area, accessible and safe, to unite the empty space that existed between the different blocks of homes situated in that part of the district. For it, and drawing inspiration from the cubist painting *Horta de Sant Joan* by Picasso, the Catalonian architects created a park with its reason for existing built into its frag-

mentized landscape. The division of space into geometric strips was made to facilitate communication and provide a more fluid connection between the many parts that extend along and throughout the park's 41 acres. In the same fashion and also thanks to the multiple axial connections within the park, the surrounding streets may be better accessed so that an open park with multiple entrances is successfully created within the neighborhood.

This idea of open space is reinforced with the creation of large open-air patios, like the old mental institution's central patio, which has been restored and integrated into the park. At the same time, pre-existing elements were also incorporated, like the Technology Conference Hall or the lake itself, which has been modified and designed to hold a new floating restaurant. The lighting is distributed into each corner of the park; notable are the huge tuning fork-shaped panels that, like large illuminating palm trees, distribute a fragmented and creative lighting design.

In both the most decorative elements and the concept of the park itself, the cubist painting Horta de Sant Joan by Picasso inspired the multiple fragmented shapes found in the park's different corners. This influence allowed for the creation of a green area between the various blocks of housing.

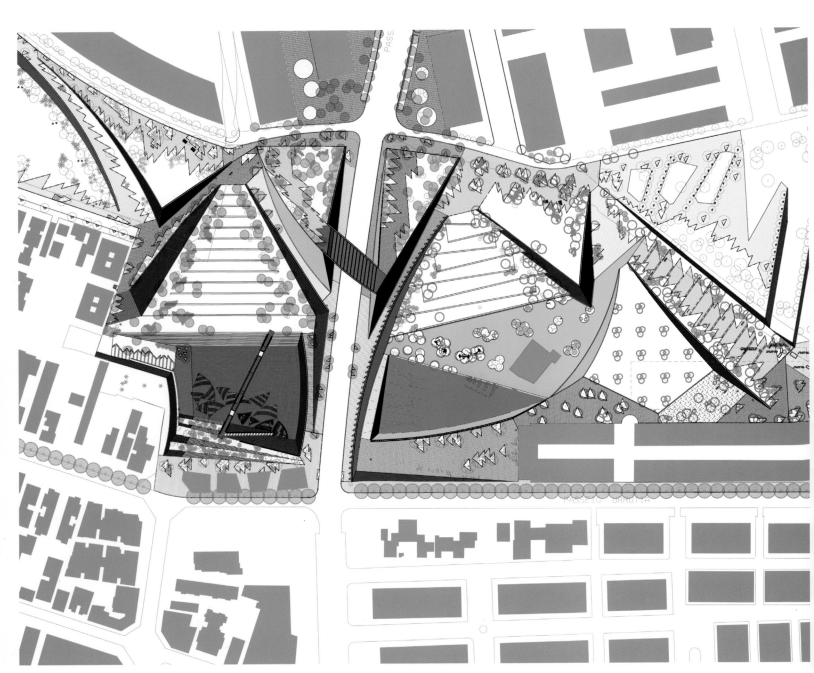

Park Plan

Square Plan

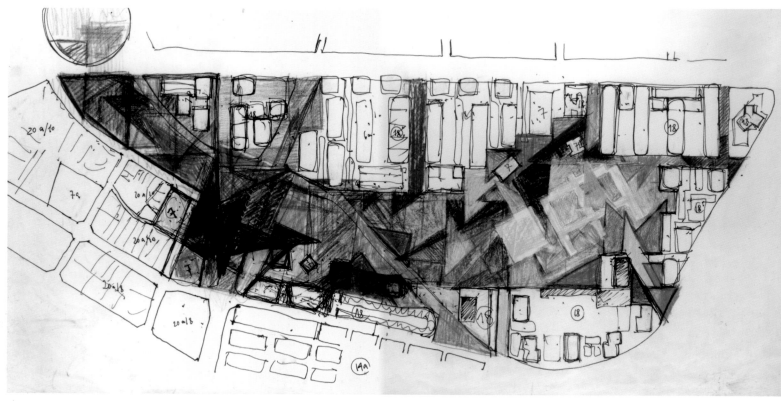

Sketch

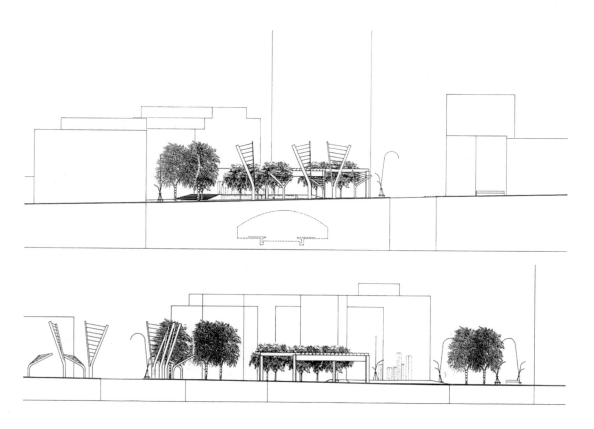

Square Sections

Photo © Gogortza & Llorella, Andrés Rodríguez

Remodeling of Joan Miró Park

Barcelona, Spain   2006

LANDSCAPE ARCHITECTS
BB & GG Arquitectes

CLIENT
Ajuntament de Barcelona

PARTNERS
*Beth Galí, Jaume Benavent, Antonio Solanas
(authors); Ruediger Wurth, Andrés Rodríguez,
Irving de la Rosa, Álvaro López, Sonia Born,
Natalia Lorenzo*

AREA
201,931 SF

COST
2,500,000 euros

The renovation of Joan Miró Park was done twenty-three years after the inauguration of the greenbelt constructed around a sculpture by the Catalonian artist. Completed by the same landscaper that designed the park over two decades ago, the intervention was necessary after the construction of a parking lot and underground rainwater tanks left behind a plot of unusable land that sits over the cement roof of the parking lot. The project cures the 64,583 square foot area of its vast emptiness while creating connections between the surrounding areas at the same time. The main idea was to create a green carpet over the cement slab that would reach Miro's statue. The huge dimension of this flowerbed makes it one of Barcelona's biggest green areas.

The regular floor plan design is shaken up a bit: the grass surface rises to form short, irregularly-shaped mounds. On this expanse, grass is combined with gramineous plants and a small amount of shrubbery, since the construction of the parking lot has actually impeded the planting of trees. Other areas have been converted into green-colored asphalt pathways that connect the interior of the park with the street.

The other part of the project entails modifications in accessibility, from the new green carpet to the main existing areas: the sculpture and the forest of pine and palm trees. The plaza itself, an esplanade of stone slightly elevated from street level and the rest of the park, connects with it by way of a staircase situated along the side that borders the new area of intervention. A metal ramp connects the plaza with the park's interior, crossing the forest of palm trees. Apart from being an alternate path beneath the shade of the trees, the ramp provides wheelchair access to the upper level.

Joan Miró Park has been subjected to a renovation owing to the construction of both an underground parking lot and a water tank. Atop these, a surface of small mounds of grass has been laid.

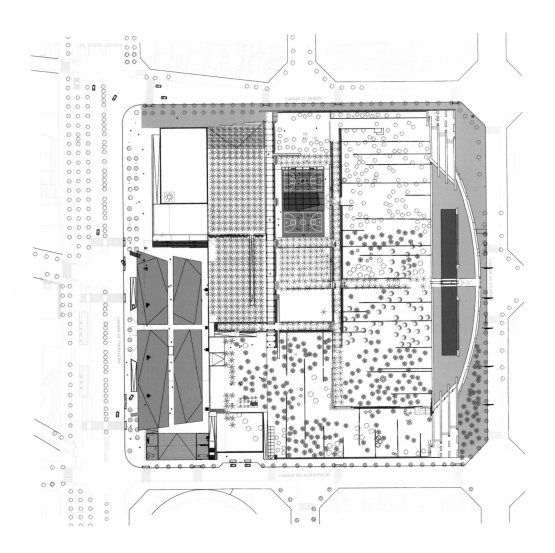

Plan

The park's renovation also consisted in connecting the existing plaza, with its sculpture by Miró, with the lower part of the newer intervention and the remaining areas. A ramp crosses the forest of palm trees, while a large staircase serves as a pedestrian walkway to the sculpture.

Park Photomontage

Ramp Photomontage

Green Area Photomontages

Photo © Catherine Mosbach

Botanical Garden of Bordeaux

Bordeaux, France   2002

LANDSCAPE ARCHITECTS

Mosbach Paysagistes

CLIENT

*City of Bordeaux, Cultural Affaires P. Richard,
Public Construction J. J. Pouguet, B. Dubos.*

PARTNERS

*N. Leroy, C. Mosbach, T. M. T. N'Guyen, J.
Saint-Chély, L. Sciascia, M. Talagrand (team);
Jourda Architects (constructor); Setec Ind, J. P.
Bonroy, L. Berger, E. Helme-Guizon, Setec Bât,
Agibat, Cholley (consultants and engineers).*

AREA

11.4 acres

The botanical gardens of Bordeaux Bastide are a center for the acclimatization of tropical plants from all over the world. Bordeaux has a long history with botanical gardens: after 1629, the city created a space dedicated solely to plants; in the following centuries the space changed locations until 2003, when it was moved definitively to an industrial area dedicated to various uses on the shores of the Garonne River. The new botanical garden creates a connection between the riverside and the center, situated on the other side of the river.

The novelty of this intervention is the dynamics of its landscape. The garden maintains its tasks of investigation and conservation while being laid out around six spaces devoted to different types of cultivation. These are arranged as a succession of gardens to soften the terrain's accentuated length. Once inside the Charente oak fence, the themes vary. The cultivated field, covering a surface of 130,350 square feet, has fields of wheat, oats, rice and flax. The gallery of the autocthonous area, distributed on 145,310 square feet, reconstructs various typical landscapes of the Aquitaine Basin: the dunes, the damp meadow, the chalky lime cliff and the swamplands. The grove of climbing plants invites one to walk through the vines and other species that use supports for cultivation. The path that navigates through the pioneer species of plants and the aquatic garden, together with the spaces pertaining to the urban garden, creates a small trip through different areas. The visitor, obliged to follow established paths, engages in a narrow relation with each environment and, little by little, assimilates the specifications of each one.

In deference to the terrain's marked length, the garden is composed of a series of six thematic spaces through which the visitor can travel by way of established routes separated by environment: a crop, a gallery that reproduces the Aquitaine Basin, a path for the pioneer species of plants, a grove for climbing plants, the aquatic and urban gardens.

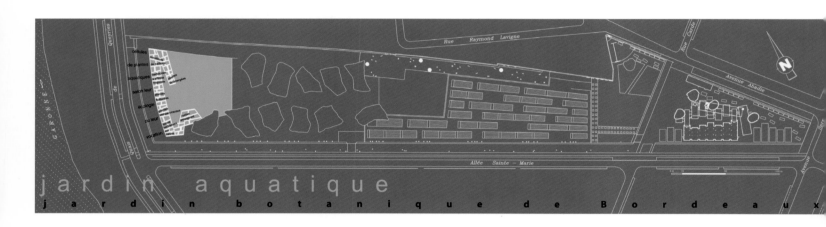

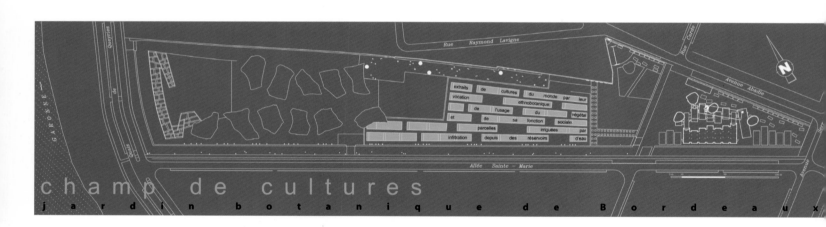

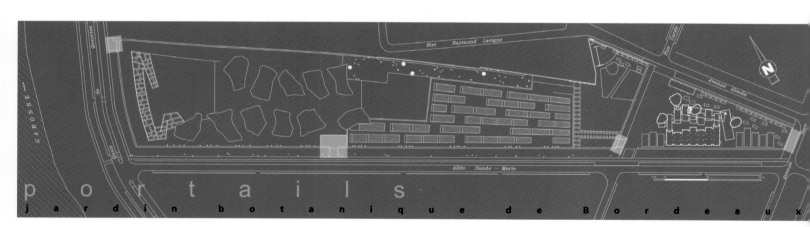

General Plans

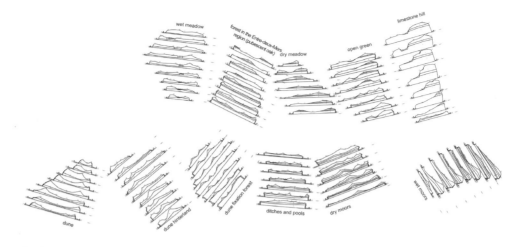

Sketch

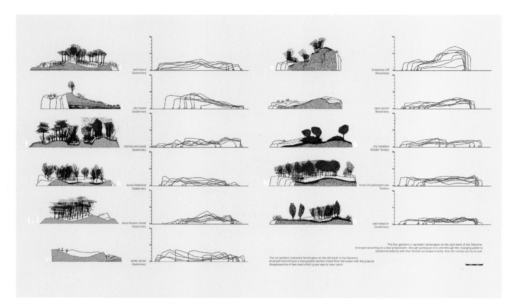

Elevations

Photo © Markus Fierz

MFO Park

Zürich, Switzerland   2002

LANDSCAPE ARCHITECTS
Burckhardt & Partner Architekten, Raderschall Landschaftsarchitekten

CLIENT
Grün Stadt Zürich

PARTNERS
Basler & Hofmann, H. Tschamper, A. Fauchère, Ch. Ritter, Th. Lanker, M. Vedruccio, P. Häfliger, U. Ress (structural engineers); Frédéric Dedelley (furniture design)

AREA
2.2 acres

Zurich's Neu Oerlikon neighborhood distinguishes itself as an industrial area that has been transformed into one of the city's liveliest areas. Recently they've built some parks, each of them characterized by a specific architecture and design. These green areas contribute to defining the neighborhood and its internal orientation, while also serving as easily recognizable places in the area. The plot where the MFO Park lies was used as a foundry waste dump for the legendary Machinefabrik Oerlikon (MFO) factory. The daunting industrial buildings make for an unconventional park that is directly inspired by the area's industrial heritage.

The park consists of two different parts, one being the continuation of the other: a square and a garden area, with the first being composed of steel architecture that serves as an impressive backdrop for climbing plants. The most peculiar aspect of this park is how they incorporated a vertical dimension: two

double, parallel structures distributed on various levels, cross over 328 feet of the main rectangle marking the open area. Visitors access the upper levels by way of stairs that take them to various places, such as a large terrace-solarium that projects towards the interior of the perimeter, balconies and vantage points that offer views of the city and the area below.

At ground level, climbing plants have been planted in relation to the metallic columns. Over time these will cover the structure completely and transform the pergola into a green wall that will be full of thousands of flowers depending on the season. To guarantee a complete, uniform coverage on the highest reaches of the structure, some plants grow out of a trench that extends throughout the entire upper perimeter, where rain gathers and serves as irrigation.

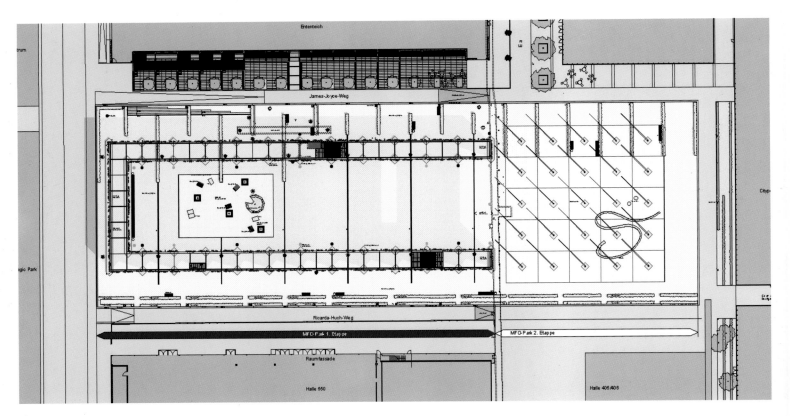

Plan

Photo © Florian Holzherr, Burger Landschaftsarchitekten, Rakete

Green Axis 13

Munich, Germany   2006

LANDSCAPE ARCHITECTS
Burger Landschaftsarchitekten

CLIENT
Maßnahmeträger München Riem GmbH

AREA
150,695 SF

COST
850,000 euros

East of Munich, on the almost 1,483 square acres of terrain that once served as an airstrip for the old Munich-Riem airport, is the small community of Messestadt Riem. As a result of the implementation of a trade fair, the so-baptized "trade fair city" has become but one more Munich neighborhood, dotted with new residential buildings, infrastructures and services. Green Axis 13 is a strip of land that runs north to south and connects the public park south of the fairgrounds with the residential area. A gravel surface planted with trees creates a green area that runs along the location's western axis.

A grove of banana trees flanks the main path, while secondary paths cross this from east to west to offer access to residents. A few walls scattered throughout the grove serve to support the long wooden benches. Counterpointing the grove area is a large field, divided into three parts by secondary paths. The southernmost part holds a transversal game park, characterized by the presence of almost a dozen large rings installed in the ground as if they were giant drops of water, fossilized at the instant they touched the ground.

The rings stand out from the grass due to their bright orange color; children's games are held within the rings. These circular cement waves have been molded into various sizes. On the westernmost side of the axis, the rhododendron bushes standing between 6.5 and 11.5 feet tall represent a continuous curtain that marks the park's border and separate it from its surroundings. On the other side of the axis, a small square-shaped island becomes a rest area shaded by a row of trees. Night lighting is confined to the main path.

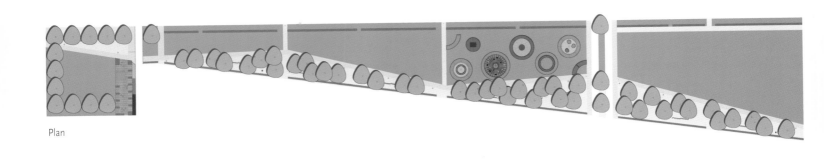

Plan

Photo © Christo Libuda, Franziska Poreski, Hutterreimann & Cejka

Landesgartenschau Wernigerode 2006

Wernigerode, Germany   2006

LANDSCAPE ARCHITECTS
*Hutterreimann & Cejka Landschaftsarchitekten,
Jens Schmahl/A Lab Architektur*

CLIENT
City of Wernigerode

PARTNERS
*Christine Orel, Christian Meyer (planting);
Bollinger & Grohmann, Wernigeröder
Ingenieurbau (engineering and construction);
IBH Ingenieurbüro Herold (civil engineering);
HGN Hydrogeologie (rehabilitation and water
management); MKR Harz-Consult (traffic
planning)*

AREA
86.5 acres

COST
8,700,000 euros

The German locality, Wernigerode, held a Gardening Fair in 2006 in a privileged area of seven lakes at the foot of the Harz Mountains that lies beside the city. The project, by Huterreimann & Cejka studios, had to conceive a park in an area surrounded by crop lands, factories and apartment blocks with no clear link. To bring the space's intrinsic qualities to the surface, a modern park was created that transcended the idea of a fair by developing a landscape that connected the lakes and preserved the area's history and identity. A long path just over half a mile long, called the "fish path," crosses the park from east to west. Tucked along the path are various architectural surprises for the visitor. These are the follies designed by Jens Schmahl of A Lab Architektur. They involve structures that revolve around water as a central and dynamic element, a source of peace and serenity: a waterfall that can be crossed, a transparent aquarium that permits observation of the breeding of fish, a lounge where marine images are projected and the simple platforms designed for rest-

ing beside the lakes and taking in the view. These points are a source of aesthetic pleasure that prolong the life and function of the park beyond its function as the setting of a show.

The main path is also a type of geological runway, the central segment of which makes use of two high limestone walls on concrete foundations along with steel bars that open towards the central lake to evoke the old mine works of the Harz Mountains. The space, previously occupied by a garbage dump, was recuperated and now holds forty thematic gardens. Various evaporating pools do the double duty of collecting rain water while avoiding the dispersion of contaminants. Meanwhile, the "recycling gardens" combine garbage and waste materials with plants to create suggestive designs. The gardens surround the "magic forest" which, in turn, is surrounded by a perforated metallic fence. The sparks it emits are a wink towards the local legends of goblins and witches from Goethe's *Faust*.

The Wernigerode Gardening Fair was the perfect inspiration behind th
creation of a modern park that would adapt to the characteristics of th
terrain. The park is laid out around a central path called the "fish path,
to which another secondary and serpentine path serves as a subtl
counterpoin

Landesgartenschau Wernigerode 2006
Ausstellungskonzept   M 1:1000

140826

Site Plan

Rendering

Photo © West 8

One North Park

Singapore, Singapore   2006

LANDSCAPE ARCHITECTS
West 8

CLIENT
JTC and National Parks Board (Singapur)

PARTNERS
Adriaan Geuze, Jerry van Eyck, Freek Boerwinkel, Marco van der Pluym, Riëtte Bosch, Glenn Scott (team); Studio Steed (associates); AUP Consultants, Rock & Waterscape Pte Ltd (consultants)

AREA
7.4 acres

COST
1,039,000 euros

In recent years, the city of Singapore has been developing one of the most ambitious programs of development and urban regeneration on the planet. The master plan for One-North, as the project is known, has been the charge of Iraqi architect Zaha Hadid and covers some 494 acres, with a high density and a complete mix of functions (commercial, academic, residential and recreational). New technology and communications play a predominant role as well. The park is conceived to be the city's green lung and is the center of the intervention, a public space without precedent that has a mission to connect the intelligent network of green zones that will make Singapore a true city-garden. It's connected to principal traffic arteries and proposes a space for contemplation, relaxation and orientation (including wireless connections at any point) for the pedestrians and cyclists who move through this busy modern architectural jungle.

Seen from the adjacent buildings, the complex looks like a multicolored serpent with a seductive and irregular topography. The park has one uninterrupted central path that alternates stretches of wood, gravel and aggregate and maintains the natural course of water through the use of bridges. It provides shaded areas throughout the entire day and has escalators to facilitate access to the highest points. Its path is full of surprising nooks and crannies; here and there we find waterfalls and pleasant fountains, always flanked by masses of colorful flowers native to the area. On a hillside, a 460 foot-long bed of water gives the impression that the water is climbing the incline. The park's water system is also designed for sustainability. The vegetation, grouped together in colorful settings, reinforces the local identity as well as the park's structure. As such, we find a forest of ficus trees, a valley of plumerias or a hill of bougainvilleas, while the beds of sansevierias trace a constant path through the park, reproduced in the structure of the benches.

The strategic placement of the park connects different points of the city and permits pedestrian and bicycle access to the main arteries. Its outline traces a green canyon that winds its way between the centrally-situated buildings. It also functions as a peaceful pond, offering tranquility to the people using the park.

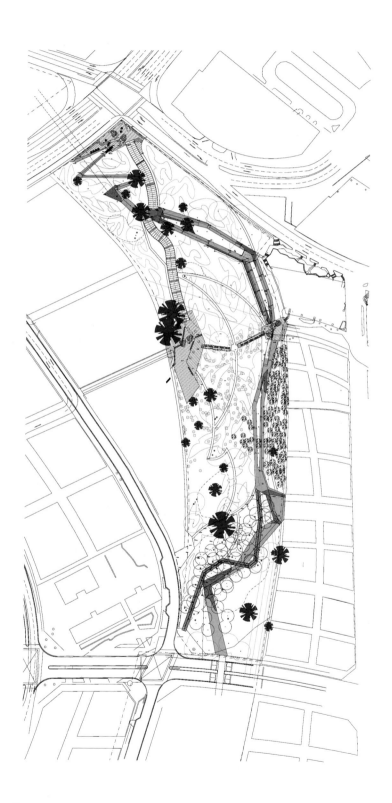

Plan

Site Plan

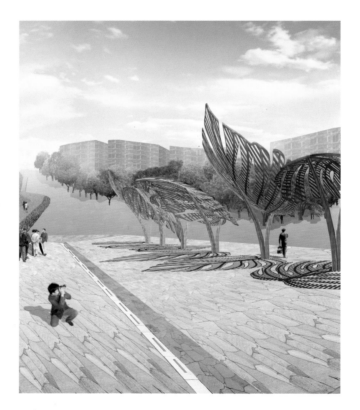

Rendering

Rendering

Photo © Yan Meng, Jiu Chen

Sungang Central Plaza

Shenzhen, China   2006

LANDSCAPE ARCHITECTS
Urbanus Architecture & Design

CLIENT
City of Shenzhen

AREA
102,257 SF

This plaza is located in Shenzhen, a city on the Pearl River delta just outside of Hong Kong. The site is surrounded by broad and busy thoroughfares. The plaza was originally planed by another firm and included a two-level 100,000-square-foot underground parking garage and a sunken plaza, along with a green area along the south side of the site. Soon after construction began, the client abandoned the original design and brought in Urbanus to redesign the above-grade areas while continuing on with the construction of the underground parking. The designers were then faced with the considerable constraints of the existing construction.

Urbanus determined that the original sunken plaza would be too isolated from the urban context and activity of the neighborhood. So the first step was to elevate the plaza to street level. From there they went on to animate the plaza as much as possible, to transform it into a lively place full of urban energy. Vitality, variety and exuberance are themes of this design. Although brick, used to pave the entire site, is by far the dominant

material, it is joined by just about every other conceivable material, and in a myriad of colors and combinations. The vocabulary of shapes used is also unlimited, with flowing lines predominating but contrasted by, for example, the boxy shapes of the building structures.

The designers took inspiration from the natural texture of the earth and water. They covered the entire surface of the site in one coherent skin of undulating brick-paved strips, which resemble the tides of water as it ebbs and flows. These tides flow around oasis islands randomly arranged to create pleasant and intimate enclaves against the chaotic surrounding urban environment. Each island is given its own unique character: colorful mosaic-tiled abstract forms, undulating ribbons of grass, or perhaps an amoeba-shaped canopy. They also include planting beds for flowering plants.

While shrouding the underground parking structure, the free-form of this coherent skin is also used to connect to two adjacent parcels that have been cut across by traffic.

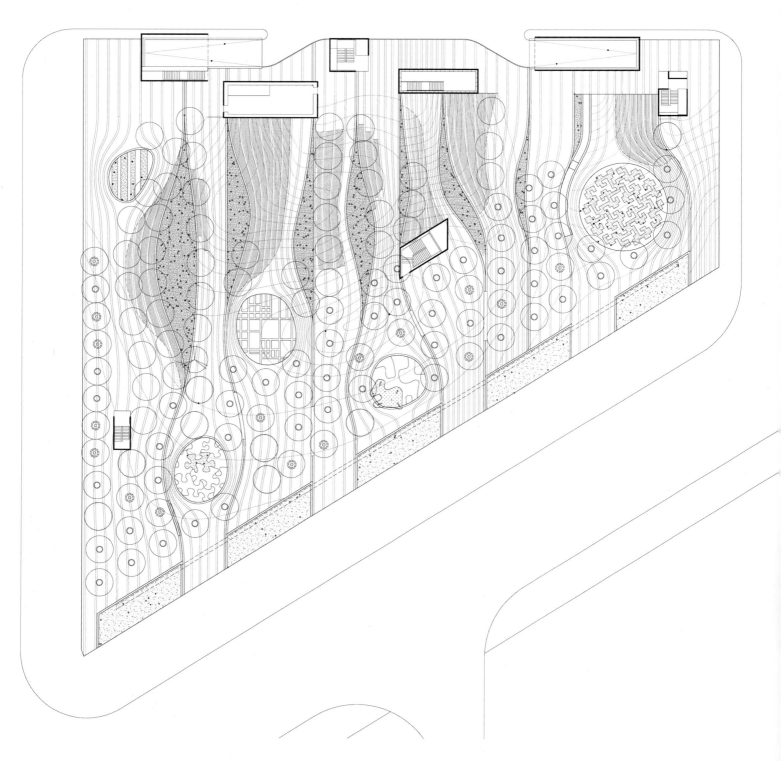

*Jigsaw puzzle shapes sheathed in brightly-colored mosaic tile, vaguel[y]
reminiscent of a swimming pool, make up one of the oasis islands tha[t]
float in the flowing lines of the brick pavement. The dynamic and chaoti[c]
urban environment presses in from all sides of this plaz[a]*

Plan

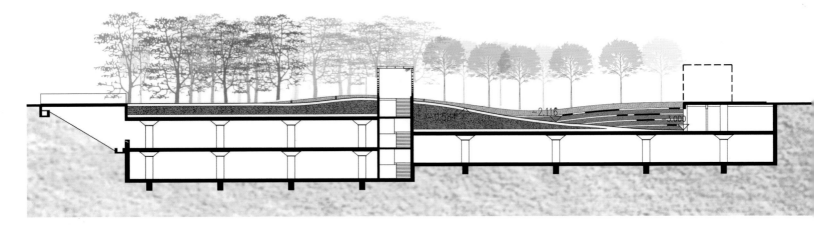

Section

Rendering

Another of the oasis islands caught in the flow of the brick paving
constructed of low steel retaining walls that hold grassy planting bed
Here the shapes are rectilinear and staccato, forming a kind of labyrint
in sharp contrast with the generally flowing shapes of the plaz

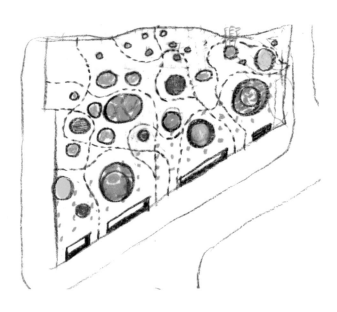

Sketch

Water Landscapes

Riversides

Waterfronts

01 Zhongshan Shipyard Park
    Zhongshan, Guangdong, China
02 Hai River Embankment Design
    Tianjin, China
03 Remodeling of River Bank
    Redon, France
04 Cendon di Silea
    Cendon di Silea, Italy
05 Welland Canal
    Welland, Canada
06 Dujiangyan Square
    Dujiangyan, China
07 Pedestrian Bridge
    Austin, TX, USA
08 HTO
    Toronto, Canada
09 Seebad Zweiern
    Buonas, Switzerland
10 Grand Plaza
    Melbourne, Australia
11 Union Point Park
    Oakland, CA, USA
12 Oriental Bay Enhancement
    Wellington, New Zealand
13 Remodeling of Rauba Capeu
    Nice, France
14 Zona de Banys Fòrum
    Barcelona, Spain
15 Ethnographic Park
    A Insua, Spain

Photo © Kongjian Yu, Yang Cao

Zhongshan Shipyard Park

Zhongshan, Guangdong, China   2002

LANDSCAPE ARCHITECTS
Turenscape

CLIENT
City of Zhongshan

PARTNERS
Kongjian Yu, Pang Wei, Huang Zhengzheng, Qiu Qingyuan, Lin Shihong (main architects and designers)

AREA
11 ha

In 1999, the local administration in Zhongshan urged for the transformation of a shipyard, closed due to lack of activity, into a public recreational area. Located on the banks of one of China's main rivers, this old industrial area has been converted into a park that not only improved the landscape of this centrally situated area, but has also given the city an opportunity for tourist attraction.

The landscapers, together with the administration, wanted the park to be a didactic occasion, with the history of the location reflected in the new design. The demolished shipyard represented fifty years of Socialist industrial history. As a witness to an era of cultural revolution, it was important to keep this memory alive. For this reason, the park has assumed a markedly industrial character, maintaining some elements of the existing industrial fabric, and is distinguished by its red and white tinged structures and architecture. Depending on the area of the park, a focus on landscape itself has been

added to the revitalization of these elements, in preparation for the planting of diverse vegetation. The mass of trees, the meadows and the bushes pruned into geometric figures all frame the architectural elements and highlight their artistic shapes.

On the riverbank, the species chosen are part of the native aquatic flora: diverse types of grass are mixed to form volumes with a certain impact for helping to understand that not only are the typical garden bushes and flora decorative, but these common and undervalued species can also achieve interesting landscape results. The park is laid out around a mirror of water connected to the river, the levels of which may fluctuate up to three feet during the day. To resolve this in particular, a system of elevated footbridges were installed that allow the area to be used at any time, independent of the actual water level. In this fashion, in order to protect the planting of some old ficus trees, a 66 foot-wide trench was constructed.

The park's design follows a functional logic: routes that unite the different elements and areas, the transformation of docks into tea houses or clubhouses and the platforms planted with vegetation native to the area. They have opted for the much-praised use of natural recyclable materials while reusing some of the industrial architecture for a didactic-recreational result.

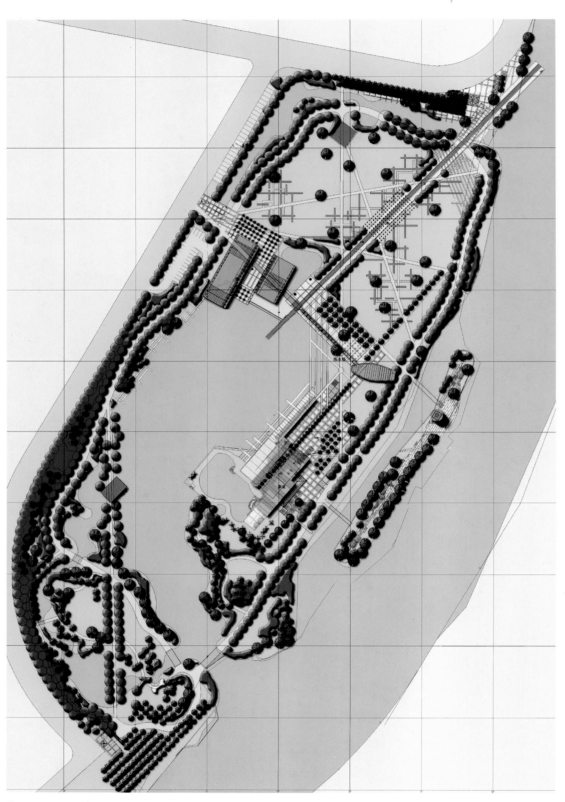

Plan

Photo © David Lloyd, Dixi Carrillo, Frank Chow/EDAW; Hai River

Hai River Embankment Design

Tianjin, China   2004

LANDSCAPE ARCHITECTS
EDAW

CLIENT
Hai Economy Development Office

AREA
3.05 miles

Since its origins, the configuration and development of the great port city of Tianjin, in the northeast of China, have been determined by the Hai River and its course. It wasn't odd then, that when the local government decided to give the city a new face, modern and cosmopolitan, in accordance with its continental relevance and its status as the economic center of the northern part of the country, they fixed their eyes on a renovation of the river's margin as the dorsal spine of the plan. The project, which would cover the rehabilitation of the 12.5 miles of the Hai River that runs through Tianjin, was designed by EDAW in four phases that corresponded with the four districts crossed by the river. Along the way, historical and cultural peculiarities were respected in each of the districts.

Phase one covers the cultural heritage area, so called for its being the area that best knew how to preserve a national identity in its physiognomy even throughout a period of colonial rule. The architects took advantage of the difference in height between the road and the river to create a space open to passersby but closed to traffic and urban hubbub; a place to incite leisure and rest while clearing the adjacent streets of cyclists. This difference in height was also smartly used to create new perspectives of historic buildings that were previously hidden. Although contemporary, the language employed in the construction of this sober modular system is also respectful, combining old stones from the river bed with the traditional slabs of grayish stone, also of local origin and designed specifically for this project.

The intervention was not conceived as a finished product; instead it attempts to make the shoreline a dynamic setting to facilitate the continuous implementation of new elements on behalf of the city and its citizens. Finished in twelve months, the new Hai River shoreline is an urban icon of Tianjin and the catalyst behind its economic growth: a visitor attraction, an engine of development and a public space capable of holding the most diverse activities throughout the year.

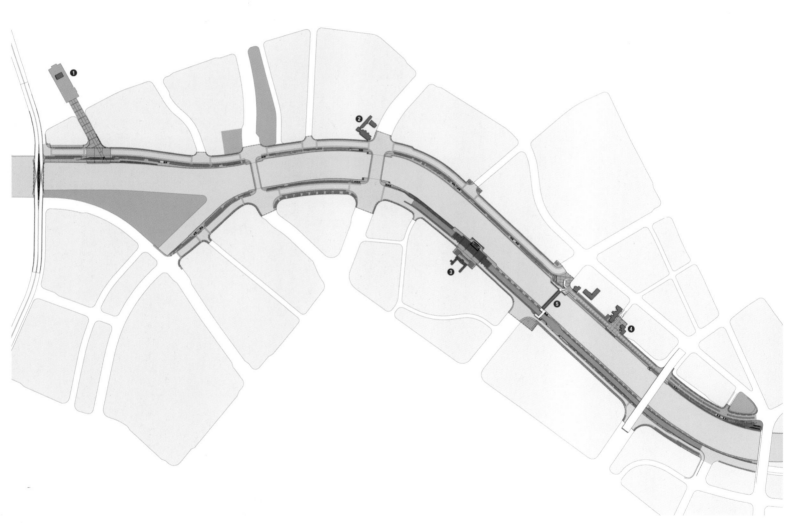

Plan

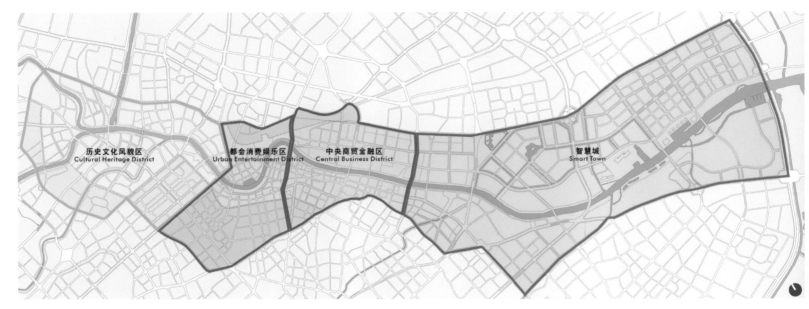

Site Plan

历史文化风貌区
Cultural Heritage District

都会消费娱乐区
Urban Entertainment District

中央商贸金融区
Central Business District

智慧城
Smart Town

Photo © Hiromi Kashiwagi

Remodeling of River Bank

Redon, France   2004

LANDSCAPE ARCHITECTS
Pierre Lafon

CLIENT
*Institut d'Aménagement de la Vilaine
Partners: Charles Carsignol/BET CERT
(engineering); Gabriel Chauvel (planting)*

AREA
26,910 SF

COST
1,623,600 euros

The widening of the road, constructed to reduce traffic through the center of a town called Redon, caused the disappearance of a tow path that bordered the Vilaine River. The execution of this project needed to achieve a double objective: on the one hand, recuperate the tow path and, on the other, prevent the floods caused by river swelling. This last objective determined the project's maximum height, in accordance with the highest recorded level of flooding plus a few centimeters for safety's sake. The elements developed along the 778 feet of affected coastline are a 328-foot-long pedestrian walkway and a bicycle lane supported by a mobile protection device in case of the river rising.

The architect in charge of the project always maintained a respect for the area's morphology in an attempt to avoid any break from the curves of the riverbank. Each of the intervention's transversal layers is independent of the rest and the distinctions between

them are achieved through strips of minerals and vegetation. This way, the bicycle lane finds its natural placement beside the road while remaining slightly elevated over it. Made with black cement and supported by another structure made of green-black cement that functions as a dry dock, the bicycle lane surface serves as support for two protective barriers: one of wood on the side nearest the road and another of galvanized steel on the other side.

Situated at the lowest height, the pedestrian walkway presents a curvature in accordance with the location's morphology; once again, the material chosen was cement, this time polished to highlight the dock's mineral aspect. The method used in pouring the cement achieved a better respect for the architectural shapes and provides sufficient flexibility for further retouches. Polygonum buckwheat, planted between the pedestrian walkway and the bicycle lane, contributes to the stability of the seashore.

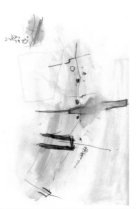

Conceptual Artwork

Photo © Adriano Marangon, Corrado Picco

Cendon di Silea

Cendon di Silea, Italy   2005

LANDSCAPE ARCHITECTS
Made Associati Architettura e Paesaggio

CLIENT
Municipal Administration of Silea

PARTNERS
Adriano Marangon, Michela De Poli (design)

AREA
86,111 SF

This project, created in the Italian district of Cendon di Silea, in Treviso, was started in 2001 and finished in 2004, six years after receiving first prize in the contest held by municipal administration to remediate and increase the value of the urban center's riverfront. The intervention offers a reworking of the space and a reorganization that recuperates traditional elements—scenic as well as historic—in the location that were barely taken advantage of until then. At the same time, the plan creates a new public space for the city's inhabitants, an area that opens to the river and connects it to the urban center. Rows of bushes and autochthonous vegetation were used to "deconstruct" the riverfront's elements and spaces. A small series of settings were created to attend to three basic premises.

The first of these is the differentiation of various relations between the user and the river itself, relations that function on different levels of perception. A renovated pier returns the area to its function as an operating riverfront by allowing small boats to dock on it, the series of platforms that constitute the pier, situated 24 inches above water level, serve as a balcony. The result is a play between different scales that offers visitors an attractive array of perspectives.

Second, the stone-covered pavement extends the path's possibilities and also serves as a link to adjacent areas. Thanks to this, a nearby social center, a small square, the church sacristy and a green area are all integrated together. The design upholds a desire to maintain the continuity between these different spaces that reach the Sile River. Last, the selection of materials like wood, steel and stone, along with the careful rustic appearance, all contribute to the project's integration into its riverside surroundings.

The simplicity of the materials chosen for the intervention, like stone, steel,
wood and the rustic finish all enable the project's discreet integration into
the Sile riverfront. Also integrated into this use of practical materials are a
social center, a small square, a church sacristy and a green area

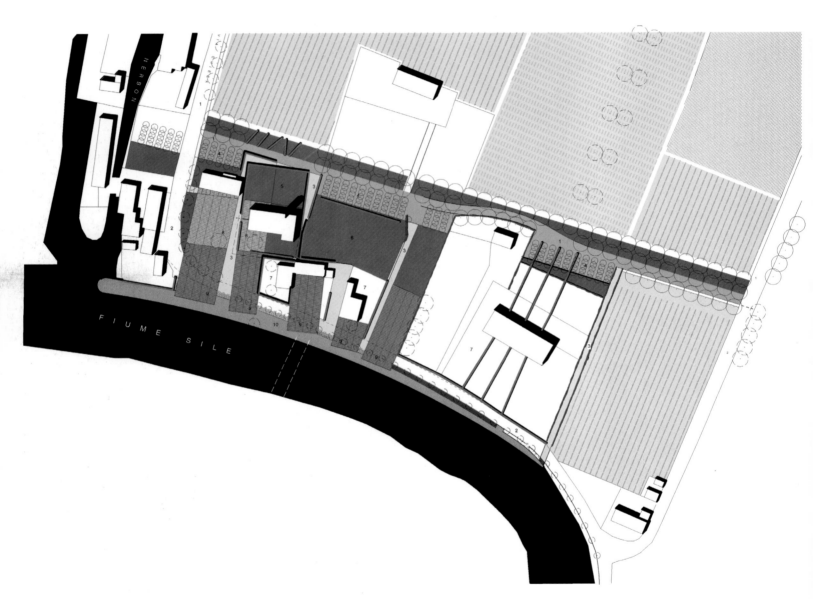

Plan

Model

A series of wooden platforms returns the riverfront to its function as a port for small boats to dock on and creates a balcony from which to view the panoramic river setting and its surroundings. This relation between the visitors and the river is created thanks to a play between different scales and situations that offer the user multiple perspectives.

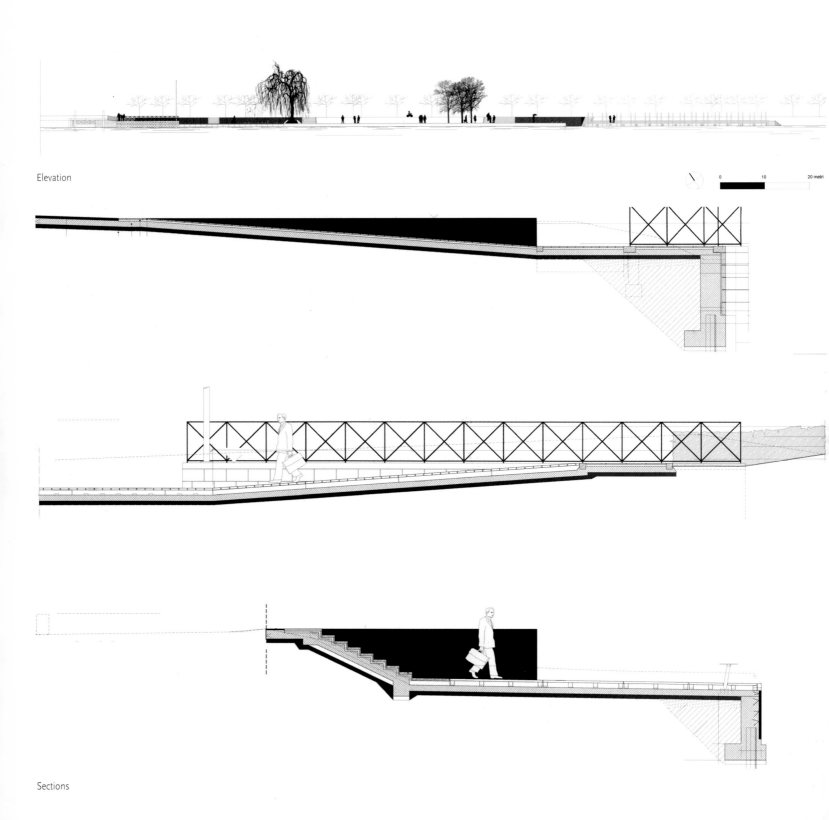

Elevation

0   10   20 metri

Sections

Photo © Neil Fox

Welland Canal

Welland, Canada   2005

LANDSCAPE ARCHITECTS
Janet Rosenberg & Associates, CS&P Architects

CLIENT
City of Welland

PARTNERS
Yolles Engineers Consultants, Merber Corporation, Martin Engineering (consultants); Rankin Construction (general contractor)

AREA
1.5 acres

COST
610,500 euros

This project sits on the bank of the historic Welland Canal, in Welland Ontario. Welland is a midsize city in the great lakes region of Ontario near Niagara Falls, and sits astride the canal at a point where major rail lines cross it. The Welland Canal is an important link on the Saint Lawrence Seaway that allows ships to avoid Niagara Falls. The historic portion of the canal where this project is located was abandoned for shipping purposes in 1972.

The program for this park is part of a larger plan for a new civic square and canal-side park to revitalize downtown Welland. The project posed a unique challenge requiring the connection of two distinct functions and faces of the site, one of which is the public square facing a main city artery, and the other is the public space connecting to the canal lands. The design approach for the Welland Civic Square and parkland area focused on creating linkages and pathways from the historic canal lands back to the heart of the city through the re-organization of the public space. Pedestrian circulation, including universal access to all areas on the site, was of prime importance. A series of ramps, bridges and viewing platforms are designed to draw people out from water's edge and onto the canal.

Strategically placed galvanized iron walkways hover over the former walls of the canal, recalling and celebrating the industrial history of Welland. Plantings include masses of Rosa rugosa to reinforce Welland's title as "The City of Roses." Beds of natural prairie grasses recall the area's natural history. Two short pedestrian piers extend out onto the historic canal.

Since its rejuvenation the downtown canal area of Welland is full of activity, with people fishing, walking, boating, and, in the winter, ice skating. The new civic space supports community events and celebrations, as well as a farmer's market. The landscape design for the Welland Canal addresses heritage issues while also addressing the changing social needs of the community. Through landscape design the site was transformed into a space to celebrate daily local events and the larger regional community.

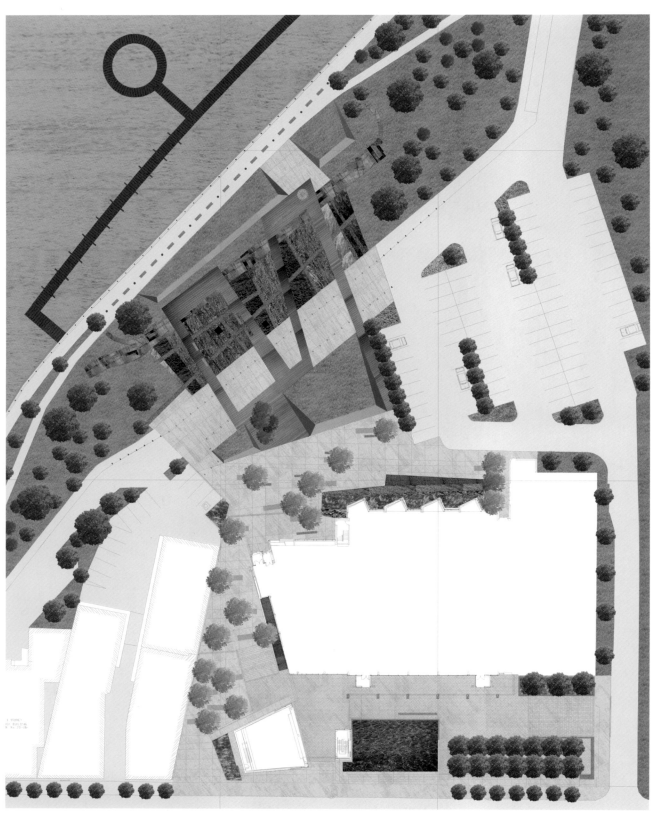

The heavy stonework of the historic canal wall is spanned by galvanized steel pedestrian bridges. Plantings of rose bushes celebrate "The City of Roses" while ornamental grasses recall the area's natural history. These connecting paths are designed to draw residents down to the water's edge.

Plan

Photo © Kongjian Yu, Cao Yang

Dujiangyan Square

Dujiangyan, China   2002

LANDSCAPE ARCHITECTS
Turenscape

CLIENT
City of Dujiangyan

PARTNERS
The Planning Bureau

AREA
27.2 acres

COST
3,392,000 euros

Dujiangyan square, covering 27 acres, is located in the middle of the monotonous landscape of the city of Dujiangyan, province of Schian, in China. Two thousand years ago, huge irrigation projects were instated in the region. With the construction of a dam that today is declared a piece of world heritage, a canal system and structures called fish mouths, constructed of bamboo and stones, the life and landscape of the region was transformed. In 1999, an international contest was held to determine the square's redesign. The winning project, executed at the tail end of 2002, was inspired by the countryside, irrigation and the local lifestyles of the area. With a low budget of less than forty dollars per 10 square feet, an urban art space was created where old histories are told in a modern language; the local and regional identities are expressed with a new focus. Satisfying the citizen's necessities and attracting more tourism was kept in mind as well.

Being bound to the middle of an urban area, the design faced many challenges. The first was the integration of a main avenue that crossed the area from north to south. The solution was to create a subterranean passage in association with areas of water excavated in a way that both sides would be united. The axis of the design is the combination of a central sculpture, three illuminated columns, a stone wall with 328 foot-long engravings, water areas and a serpentine stream that comes out along the top of the axis. Beside the axis, a diagonal line visually connects the pedestrian walkways and points towards the valley a few miles north where the famous dam is located.

The central sculpture of granite and jade, 98 feet-high by 10 feet-wide, pays homage to the goddess of the river. Among the artistic pieces is a metallic gold canopy supported by bronze poles that evokes the wooden triads used for the old irrigation system. The rest of the space is designed in conjunction with its users: included are areas for card tables, a favorite pastime of the city's inhabitants. An amphitheater and three areas of water were designed so that visitors would interact.

*The space is defined by art pieces integrated into the daily usage of th
square. One of these, this metallic gold canopy supported by bronze pole
recalls old irrigation tools. The 98 foot-high central sculpture is constructe
of granite and functions as the design's focal point. At its base, a whirlpo
functions as a fountain and a waterfall (see following pages,*

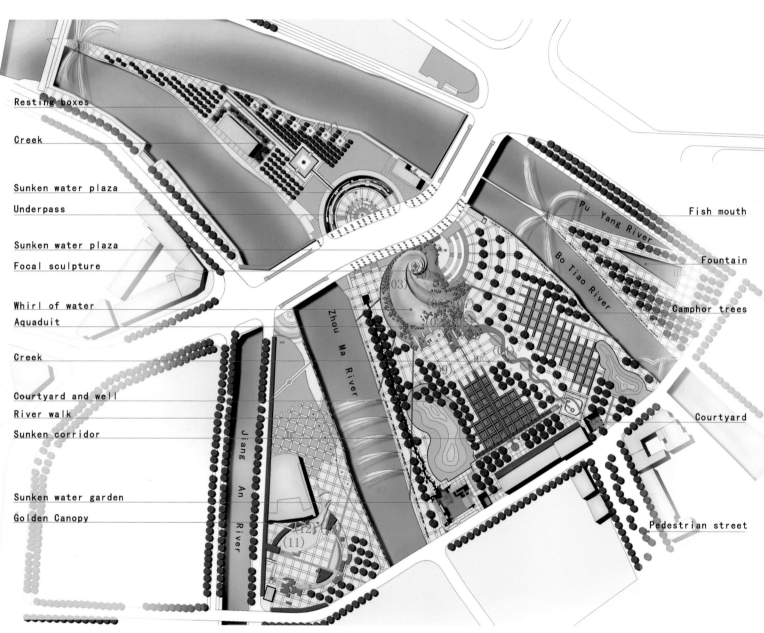

Resting boxes

Creek

Sunken water plaza
Underpass

Sunken water plaza
Focal sculpture

Whirl of water
Aquaduit

Creek

Courtyard and well
River walk
Sunken corridor

Sunken water garden
Golden Canopy

Pu Yang River

Bo Tiao River

Zhou Ma River

Jiang An River

Fish mouth

Fountain

Camphor trees

Courtyard

Pedestrian street

Plan

Photo © Paul Finkel/Pistol Design

Pedestrian Bridge

Austin, TX, USA   2005

LANDSCAPE ARCHITECTS
Miró Rivera Architects

CLIENT
private

PARTNERS
Juan Miró (principal); Chuck Naeve/Architectural Engineers Collaborative (structural engineering); David Mahler/Environmental Survey Consulting (landscape design); Rusty Signor/Signor Enterprises (contractor)

AREA
80 F

Austin Lake, in Texas, is integrated into an area of dense vegetation that holds an ecosystem as rich as it is delicate. This 79 foot-long bridge achieves its function of saving the body of water by uniting the property's main building with a recently constructed guest house. It's part of a long-term general intervention project to protect the native flora and fauna. The plan eliminates invasive species while reintroducing other native species and restoring and strengthening the marshlands; these are a meeting point along the migratory path of various birds, like egrets, cranes and swans. The pedestrian bridge is inspired by juncus and other vegetable species that grow on the lake's shore, melding into its surroundings in a surprising fashion. Also, like the paths and other infrastructural elements of the location, design was used to underline the ecosystem's fragility, so that the visitor would feel an unconscious impulse to care for and respect the surroundings.

The construction consists of an arc-shaped structure of five tubes that sustain a set of irregular length sticks made of oxidized steel, much like bamboo shoots or tree trunks that would have naturally knotted to such an extent as to have become almost invisible, camouflaged with the countryside. The absence of any treatment or finish on the material, which is exposed to bad weather, accentuates its discreet integration. The handrail consists of a cord held by various steel rings to a horizontal tube that itself is welded to the vertical bars. On each side, the metallic structure rests on two blocks of white cement. To erect the buttress ramps, slabs of stone were dug from the ground and vertically installed. The bridge also serves as a privileged scenic viewpoint; when crossing it, the visitor can stop a moment to contemplate the lake, its backdrop and the pleasant surroundings reflected in the water.

The bridge's basic structure consists of various arc-shaped tubes that cover
a 79 foot-long stretch over the lake to unite the main building with a guest
house. Aside from forming a connection between the shore sides it serves
as a viewpoint from which visitors can contemplate the surroundings.

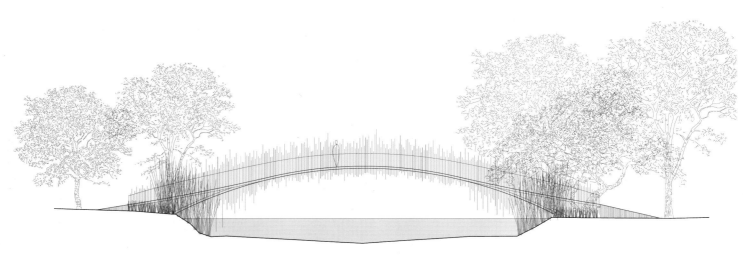

Elevation

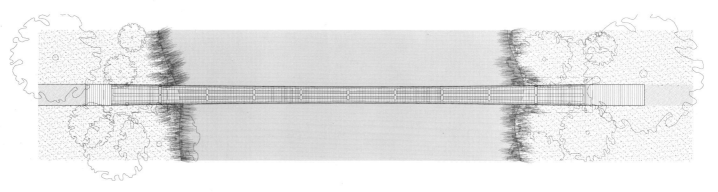

Plan

Sketch

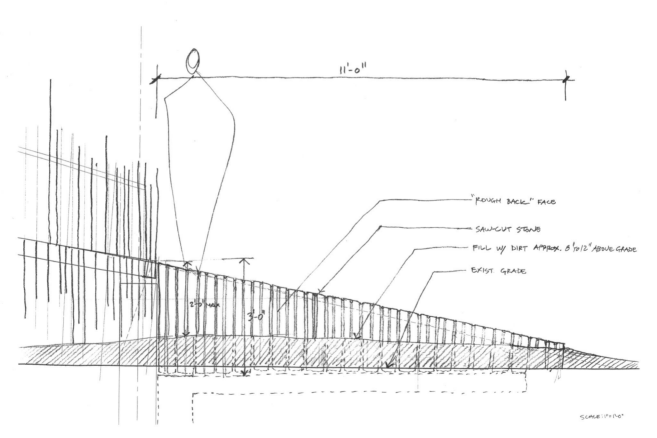

11'-0"

"ROUGH BACK" FACE

SAW-CUT STONE

FILL W/ DIRT APPROX. 8" TO 12" ABOVE GRADE

EXIST. GRADE

2'-0" MAX

3'-0"

SCALE: 1" = 1'-0"

Bridge Sketch

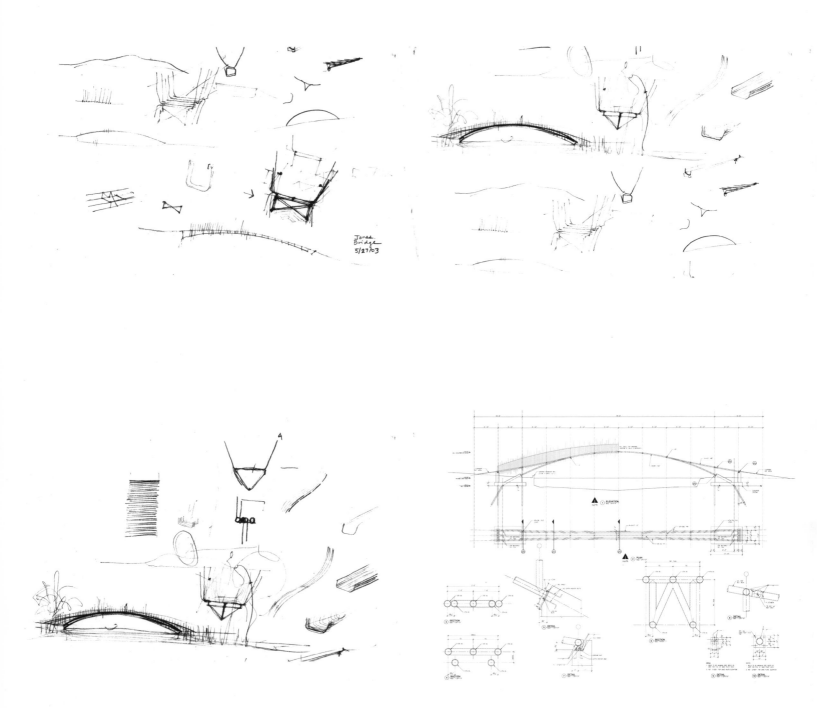

The bridge is integrated into a delicate ecosystem. This is why its shape respectfully mimics the flora around the lake, particularly the bamboo shoots. It indirectly instills in the visitor a desire to respect the fragile ecological balance. The architects were inspired by reeds which grow beside the lake

Sketches & Construction Details

Photo © Neil Fox

HTO

Toronto, Canada   2007

LANDSCAPE ARCHITECTS
Janet Rosenberg & Associates, Claude Cormier Architectes Paysagistes Inc, Hariri Pontarini Architects

CLIENT
City of Toronto

PARTNERS
Leni Schwendinger Light Projects Ltd, Sustainable Edge, Rina Greer (public art consultants); Beth Kapusta (communications consultant); William Greer (historical consultant); Somerville Construction (general contractor)

AREA
5.68 acres

COST
7,164,300 euros

The opening of HTO Park signifies the start of revitalization efforts of the Toronto riverfront and a change in perception on behalf of its citizens. The project is inserted into a larger strategic plan pushed by local government to create new public spaces from about two and a half acres of riverfront property. The city wanted to reclaim a connection with Lake Ontario through a series of green recreational areas: parks, paths and public areas. The result achieved by the team of Canadian architects is a unique place, flexible and functional, a meeting point for entertainment and relaxation.

Located in terrain previously damaged by intense industrial use, the project suggests a type of green area with an urban beach. While its name derives from the chemical formula for water, H_2O, its design is inspired by a famous painting from the impressionist Georges Seurat, *La Grande*

Jatte. It depicts an evening of recreation beside the water; the idea was to reproduce this same scene, leave the city behind and offer an oasis of entertainment by the water. On the two plots where the park was developed, separated by a dock, what is seen and heard is water, though a perception of the city reminds visitors that they are no longer in natural surroundings but on an urban beach. The elements that mark the park's design are irregular hills of grass, which create a permeable barrier between the construction and the water, a beach of sand, a path beside the lake and a dozen yellow metallic sunshades planted into the sand. These last items have become a city icon; their bright color makes them visible from various points of the city. The park has successfully eliminated the barrier between the city and the lake.

*Planted with willows and maple trees, the green hills occupy the majority
of the surface area. The wooden path and the bright sunshades planted in
the sand beside the water provide the park with a beach-type character
that pushes the city into the background.*

Plan

Photo © Stefan Koepfli

Seebad Zweiern

Buonas, Switzerland   2004

LANDSCAPE ARCHITECTS
Koepfli Partner Landschafsarchitekten

CLIENT
Municipality of Risch

AREA
29,063 SF

COST
65,000 euros

Lake Zug, located in the central region of Switzerland, has an old bathing spot that was traditionally used by inhabitants of the area. The recent approval of a series of legal rules for these types of spas forced its reform and adjustment with an eye towards guaranteeing the safety of the bathers. Given the beauty of the surroundings, the intervention had to be as discreet and restricted as possible in order to preserve its proverbial idyllic and serene atmosphere. With this premise in mind, work started with the knocking down of the long wall that ran around the perimeter of the lake, since it made access to the shore from the water dangerous and difficult. To rectify this circumstance, the terrain was partially flattened and the wall was replaced with an inclined surface that descends in a very slight slope towards the lake. Following this, and with the intention of compensating for a strip of grass that was lost to this design, the pavement was covered with a layer of gravel that serves as a transition from water to grassy area.

The remaining parts of the wall were covered with a series of wooden terraces with sandboxes for the children to play in. Respecting the original layout of the area, and the uses typical to it, various wooden platforms were placed only a few feet from the shore. These provide excellent views of the lake, the nearby villages and the impressive mountains. To one side of the artificial beach, a small wooden pier is placed in the water; on the other side, a platform accessible from the water by a wooden ladder is in deep enough water to permit diving. The use of natural materials, like wood and gravel, responds to a directive aimed at reducing to a minimum any aesthetic disturbance of the area. The elements chosen for the fixtures reinforce a delicate and light sensation.

The Seebad Zweiern bathing area was redesigned with an eye toward adapting to new legal rules for spas. The materials used for the intervention, gravel and wood, are discreetly integrated into the natural surroundings. A pebble beach and various wooden platforms replace the original wall

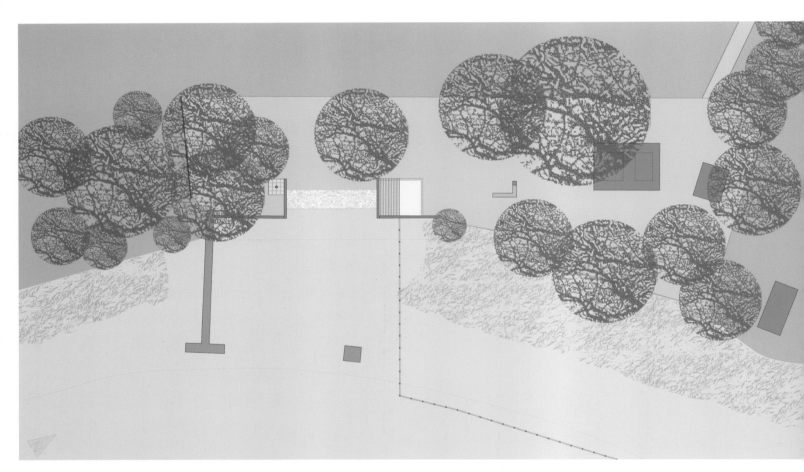

Plan

Photo © David Simmonds

Grand Plaza

Melbourne, Australia   2004

LANDSCAPE ARCHITECTS
Rush & Wright Associates, Ashton Raggatt McDougall Architects

CLIENT
Docklands Authority, Vicurbant

PARTNERS
Connell Mott McDonald (engineering); ARUP (service engineering); Vision Design (lighting design); Cat McCleod, Michael Bellemo, John Kely (artists)

AREA
376,737 SF

COST
12,475,800 euros

Harbour Esplanade is the name of a gigantic project aimed at transforming the great port esplanade of Melbourne—where the docklands were previously located—into an area of urbanization. The area's industrial profile has given way to a burgeoning urban district shared by huge movie studios, residential apartments, plazas, parks and open-air exposition spaces. To rehabilitate this long sector, which runs along 1.2 miles of the bay from north to south, the work was conceived with the idea of horizontality, providing various connected public spaces.

The nucleus of the urban stretch is constituted by the 1,640-foot-long Grand Plaza, a public forum that definitively links the center of Melbourne to this port area. It's ingenious and colorful design emphasizes the east-west spatial connection through lines painted in the pavement; at the same time, these evoke the former order of the old merchant containers and markets. This design serves to take visual impact from the roadways that cross the plaza while helping to

delineate, with the help of vegetation, the different spaces and their functions. For this, native species were planted, like palm trees, fig trees and eucalyptus lemon trees that separate the pedestrian walkways from passing traffic. These tree walls create an agreeable microclimate for passersby and serve as protection against the strong winds blowing in the area.

Keeping in mind the system's sustainability and care for the environment, the green areas are irrigated with modern sprinkler systems designed to take advantage of rainwater. The plaza has also been conceived to hold artistic and cultural offerings for the public, including open-air shows of significant works. One example is the *Shoal Fly By* sculpture by artists Michael Bellemo and Cat Macleod. Lastly, special attention has been given to the night lighting; a balance was sought between the general atmosphere and the scenic effects that emphasize the plaza's original urban fixtures.

*The design of the Grand Plaza and the Harbour Esplanade underlines th
horizontality that has characterized this coastal area throughout i
history. The different colors of the surface, the materials chosen and th
trees serve to rationally distribute the space and its function*

Site Plan

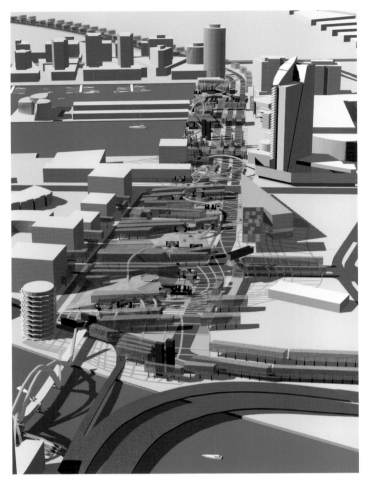

Perspective

Photo © David Goldberg, Dixi Carrillo, Proehl Studio

Union Point Park

Oakland, CA, USA   2005

LANDSCAPE ARCHITECTS
Grupo de Diseño Urbano

CLIENT
The Unity Council

PARTNERS
Mario Schjetnan (director); Alejandro Lira, Yara Sigler, Juan Carlos Guerra, Alma Du Solier (others); Chris Patillo/Patillo & Garret Associates (project development)

AREA
11 acres

Like many other recently rehabilitated coastal areas throughout the cities of the world, Union Point Park sits on what used to be a shipyard. These nine acres are part of a general plan attempting to configure a network of parks and paths that, situated along the San Francisco bay, would facilitate public access to an area that was once primarily industrial. The park offers services to Fruitvale and San Antonio, the two neighborhoods with the highest population of children: the ones who most need an open recreational space.

The clients required that the master plans of the EDAW firm be respected, which is why Mario Schjetnan, of GDU studios, and PGA Design maintained the marine pathway, the recreational and natural areas and the installation of entryways and parking spots. Nevertheless, they accented the nearby mounds to convert them into hills that could then be united by bridges. This way, not only is protection from wind and traffic guaranteed, but a pedestrian walkway and a bicycle lane could also be created with views of the city, the estuary and the sea itself. The most pronounced hill, 23 feet high, is Union Point Hill, which becomes the main entryway. It's a well-rounded shape, ancestral while remaining contemporary, covered by a spiral that culminates in a steel mast that holds a metallic pergola over the park with the help of supporting cables. The hill and the mast are lit at night like a lighthouse.

The park also has some original shelters installed over the picnic areas. The little pebble mounds that hold the shelters in place evoke the surrounding seascape. A pier connects the marina, on the one side, with the recreational area and the parking lot on the other side. Halfway between is the so-called ceremonial circle and an environmental sculpture by artist Ned Kahn that pays homage to the cyclical nature of the waves and tides. Last, the parking area is an ellipse delineated by a group of trees that form a sort of vestibule facing the sea.

The park provides the services required for the youth population with open
recreational spaces. Protection against the wind, already provided by hills
is intensified in the picnic areas, thanks to the inclined metallic shelters

Plan

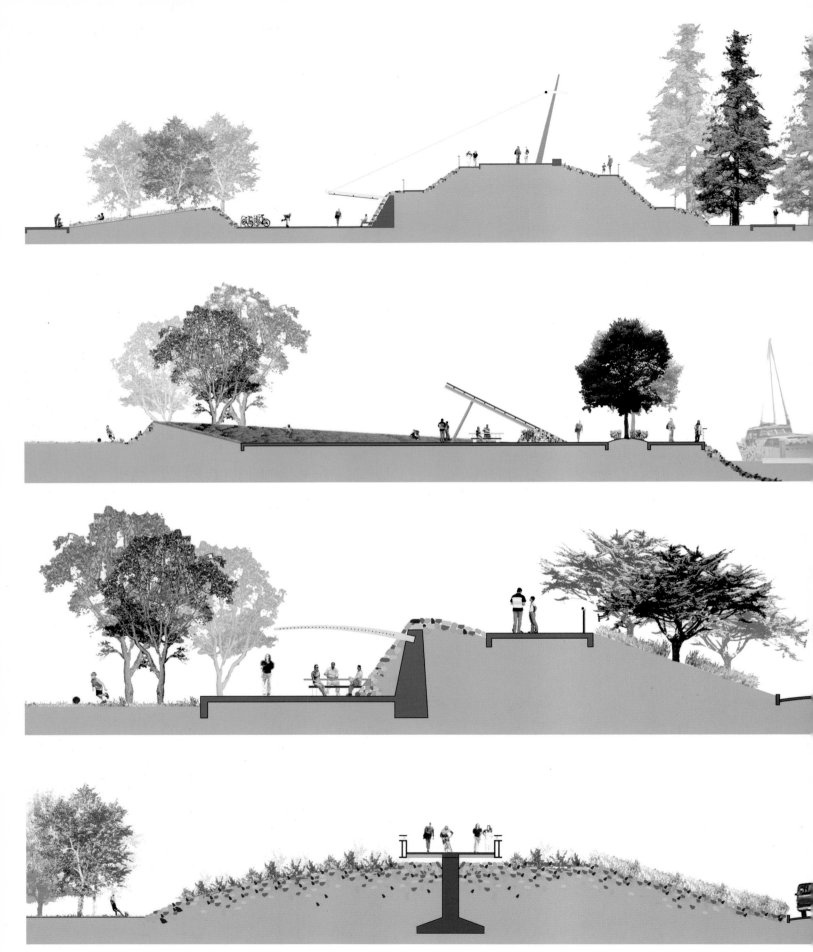

Sections

The clear geometric combinations and the environmental consideration
create, without breaking from the area's master plan, an original design
that allows for multiple functions and uses by inhabitants. The architect
followed the client's desire to respect the marine pathway and the natural
area

Model

Photo © Nik Kneale, Simon Devitt

Oriental Bay Enhancement

Wellington, New Zealand   2003

LANDSCAPE ARCHITECTS
Christopher Kelly/Architecture Workshop, David Irwin/Isthmus Group

CLIENT
Wellington City Council

PARTNERS
Ed Breeze/Tonkin & Taylor (engineering consultant)

AREA
107,639 SF

This project, from the city of Wellington, in New Zealand, was created with a dual purpose: to provide a controlling system against the strength of the sea in a particularly exposed port area and to use the occasion to offer the citizenry an area for public recreation. On the one hand, the old tidebreakers were replaced, while on the other hand, an attempt was made to give the area a stronger geographical relief. The project saw the participation of not only landscapers, but civil and coastal engineers as well, who proved indispensable in dealing with the plan's complexity. The rehabilitated area is the space between the beach and the port where ships come to dock. The division between the two areas is clear and the project needed to find a way of maintaining this separation without overly disrupting the area.

The proposal resolves its technical problems with the installation of a submerged barrier, avoiding the construction of massive eyesores on the land itself. This same barrier comes to the surface to transform itself into the project's principal component: the rectangular blocks of cement combine to form a recreational area where one can sit, sunbathe, play in the pools left behind by the tide or admire the view. The dike attains a dual purpose: a barrier against waves and a place for sitting.

The project also includes a series of pedestrian walkways and ramps. A wooden footbridge unites the dike with a garden area and acts as the project's backbone. The green areas, covered with grass or trees, open out on both sides of the footbridge, the limits of which are marked by a continuous white concrete bench. The small structure that holds the bathrooms is protected by a wood laminated structure that shades the main path.

The dike was planned to comply with a dual purpose: protect the beach area from waves and provide a platform for recreation. The combined rectangular cement blocks create areas that are both intimate and communal.

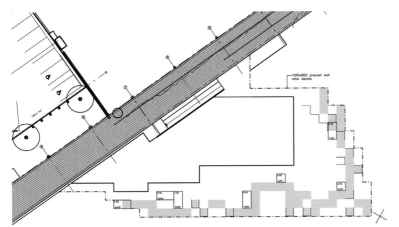

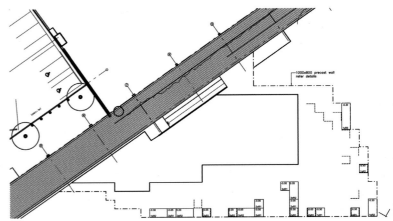

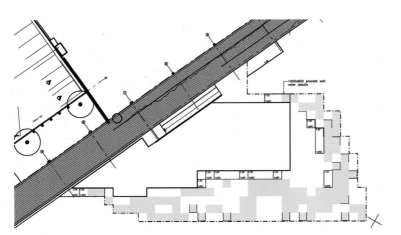

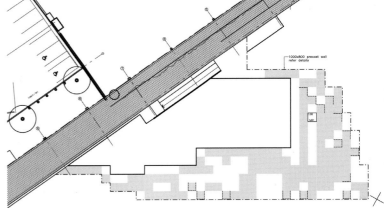

High/Low Tides Plans

Photo © Jean-Michel Landecy

Remodeling of Rauba Capeu

Nice, France   2003

LANDSCAPE ARCHITECTS
Stoa Architecture

CLIENT
Ville de Nice

PARTNERS
*Charle Bové, Thierry Ciccione, Pascal Urbain
Associés (main architects); Mariane Rougé
Benoît Campion, Direction des Espaces Publics
de la Ville de Nice, Denis Carlo, Francis
Donadey, Michel Congost (others)*

AREA
984 F

COST
1,520,000 euros

The Rauba Capeu pier connects the port of Nice with the Promenade des Anglais. The 984 foot-long road that runs along the sea continues to bend around a castle on a hilltop, offering some unique views of the Bay of Angels. This renovation project of the city's rockiest portion of seaside terrain is part of a larger frame inscribed by an overall intervention that affects the city's network of public spaces. The intentions behind the Rauba Capeu pier project is to transform a place with many possibilities from a point of departure that would begin with the prolongation of a bicycle lane that begins on the Promenade des Anglais, thus creating a long panoramic pathway.

Excavated from the rock and 43 feet above sea level, the path's space didn't offer much room for maneuvering. As a result, the planners decided to accentuate the relation between the sea and the hill instead of softening it. Not an object or tree is found between the cliffside and the rocky hillside slope: the relation with the sea is direct and without obstacle. In this sense, the interven-

tion makes use of the elements offered by the surrounding area, the orography, so to speak; the white limestone and the panoramic views.

To strengthen the impression of being on one continuous balcony, the new pathway is made along a series of stones that follows the curve of the ledge on a level slightly lower than the road above. This permits the foregoing of any barriers and, at the same time, transforms this difference in height into a continuous bench facing the sea. The two-lane bicycle path parallels the pedestrian walkway while remaining alongside the higher level of the road. The materials used create continuity with the existing layout of the connecting pier: limestone from Bourgogne for the pathway, red asphalt for the bicycle lane and black asphalt for the road. Lighting for the pedestrian walkway is assured with the use of spotlights, fitted along the bank and the low wall. The sundial, located on the bicycle lane extension, is comprised of twelve beacons that illuminate the area at night with a diffuse light.

The path that protrudes from the pier is excavated straight out of the hill-side rock. To avoid adding foreign elements to the landscape, the difference in height between the road and the pedestrian walkway has been used to create one continuous bench. The path precedes an external pedestrian walkway and a two-lane bicycle path.

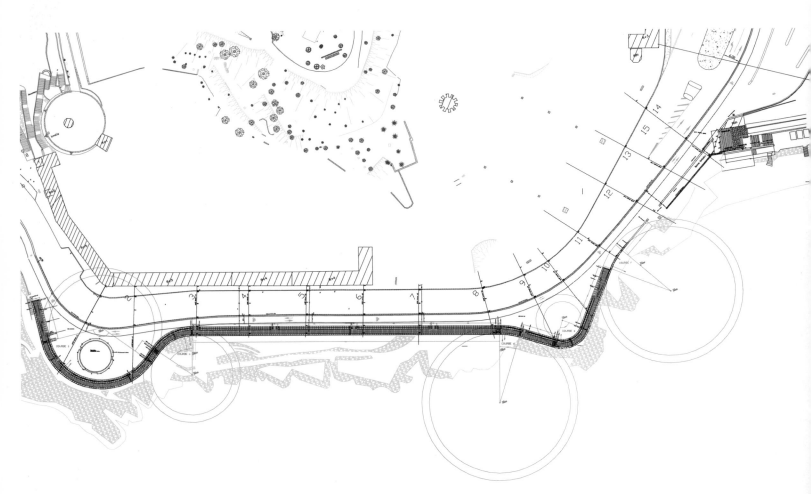

Plan

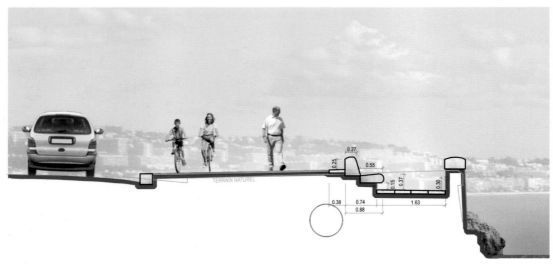

Photomontages with Sections

Detail Plan

Aerial View

Photo © Gogortza & Llorella, Andrés Rodríguez

Zona de Banys Fòrum

Barcelona, Spain   2004

LANDSCAPE ARCHITECTS
BB & GG Arquitectes

CLIENT
Ajuntament de Barcelona

PARTNERS
Beth Galí, Jaume Benavent (authors); Andrés Rodríguez (collaborator architect)

AREA
27.2 acres

COST
6,000,000 euros

The Forum Bathing Area corresponds to a part of the Barcelona coastline between the Prim Street storm drain and the leisure harbor. The project is part of the interventions made in the huge space that held the Cultural Forum in an effort to maximize its subsequent usefulness. Among its new uses are a great variety of cultural, sport and recreational activities and a capacity to hold festival celebrations and a multitude of conventions. Protected from the Levantine storms by a series of reefs, these pools of salt water are conceived as a calm and controlled alternative to the natural beaches of the coastal seaboard of Barcelona.

The coast projects 5 feet out into the sea, like a stone wall, and from that point a staircase descends into the water to a depth of about 4 feet. From within the water emerge various pillars, in a row, which serve the double purpose of framing the horizon and signifying the safe swimming area and differentiating it from the open sea. Beside the jetty, flanked by a dock and some white marble-covered platforms, is an artificial beach on a slight incline that diminishes the drop by 2.5 feet The marble platforms function as small islands and go out deep enough to permit diving. Deck chairs, tables, ramps and showers, all made of cement, configure an architectural base that protects the beach from harsh weather.

Halfway between the water and the coast they have shaped a cavity, formed by the solid concrete wall, which resembles a huge hand hugging a strip of sea. Access to its interior is gained from the sea and the visible jets of water form part of this body of water's renovation plans and its overall circulation. The intervention's next objective is the treatment of this sea water, as of now only controlled for bathing, with an eye towards offering thalassotherapy services in a to be planned in the future thermal park.

This intervention has permitted the creation of new beaches along th
Barcelona seaboard: Levante Beach and the bath area. A series of artificic
reefs protects the latter beach from storms. The bath area brings the se
closer to the Forum esplanade and creates an aquatic activity area tha
intertwines with the leisure harbo

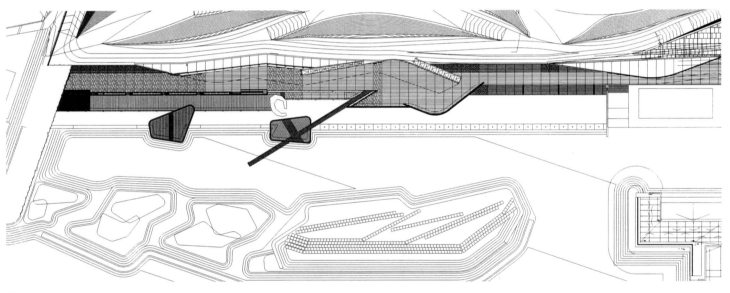

Plan

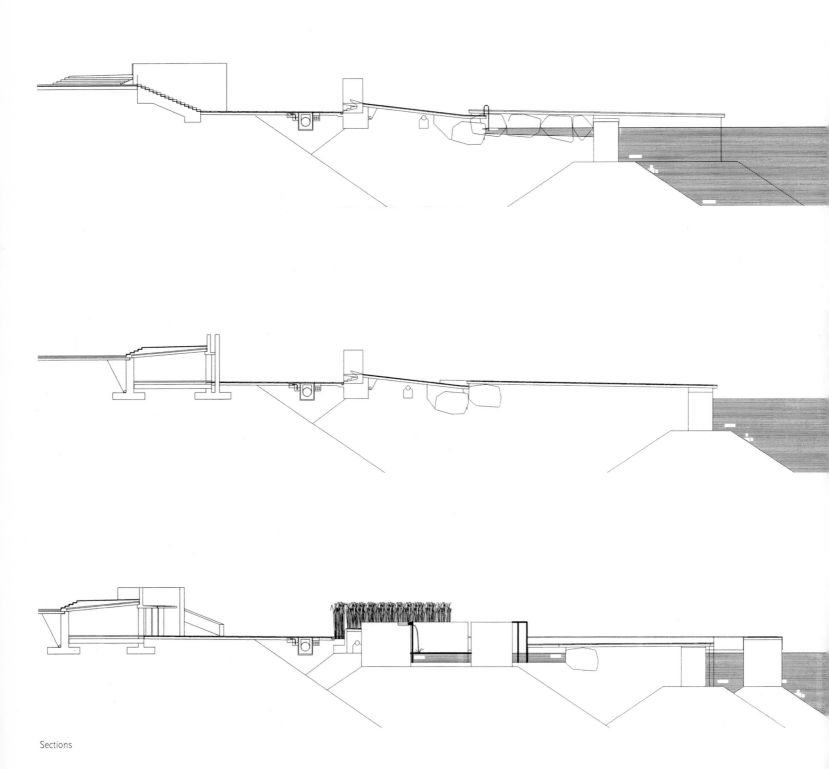

Sections

Photo © Juan Rodríguez

Ethnographic Park

A Insua, Spain   2002

LANDSCAPE ARCHITECTS
Estudio Felipe Peña & Francisco Novoa

CLIENT
Ayuntamiento de Viveiro, Demarcación de Costas de Galicia

PARTNERS
José Miguel Estevan Dols (engineering); Probisa (constructor)

AREA
243,081 SF

COST
1,868,500 euros

After having seen the results of the old iron ore loading platform on the ria of Viveiro, the Galician authorities decided to transform this place of industrial archaeology into a cultural space of entertainment, leisure and learning. The reform project and the construction of the newer structures were based on reflections of the locale's historic past. This theoretical analysis brought the architects to decide on recuperating the industrial remains and turning them into places of interest.

The old loading platform is located in an attractive spot on the Galician coast, on a small peninsula notable for morphological and cultural peculiarities that make it especially interesting. The terrain's strong incline towards the sea and its nonlinearity made designing this public space for strolling and resting very difficult. From the access area to the lower scenic viewpoint that touches the water, the incline was substantial and finally resolved with a vertical path of alternating stairways and platforms. Continuity with a path from the nearby town of Covas was insured by another path that, once finished, would connect the beach with A Insua.

The ruins of the mining structures have been transformed into an area for temporary residence and an ethnographic park: the activities are related to the observation of the landscape and the history of the dock. The structures were conditioned to meet two criteria: as archaeological remains and as new architectural elements that evoke and suggest pre-existing structures. Another characteristic component of the project is the repeated structural element that recalls the metal loading platform that would approach the docking boats. This structure is crowned at its highest point by the walls of the chutes, surrounded by turf vegetation and some trees.

The A Insua complex incorporates structural elements from the o
loading dock, standing since 1899. Its new function compris
entertainment and cultural activities, taking advantage of the o
industrial remains and adding new elements of construction to ther

Plan & Site Plan

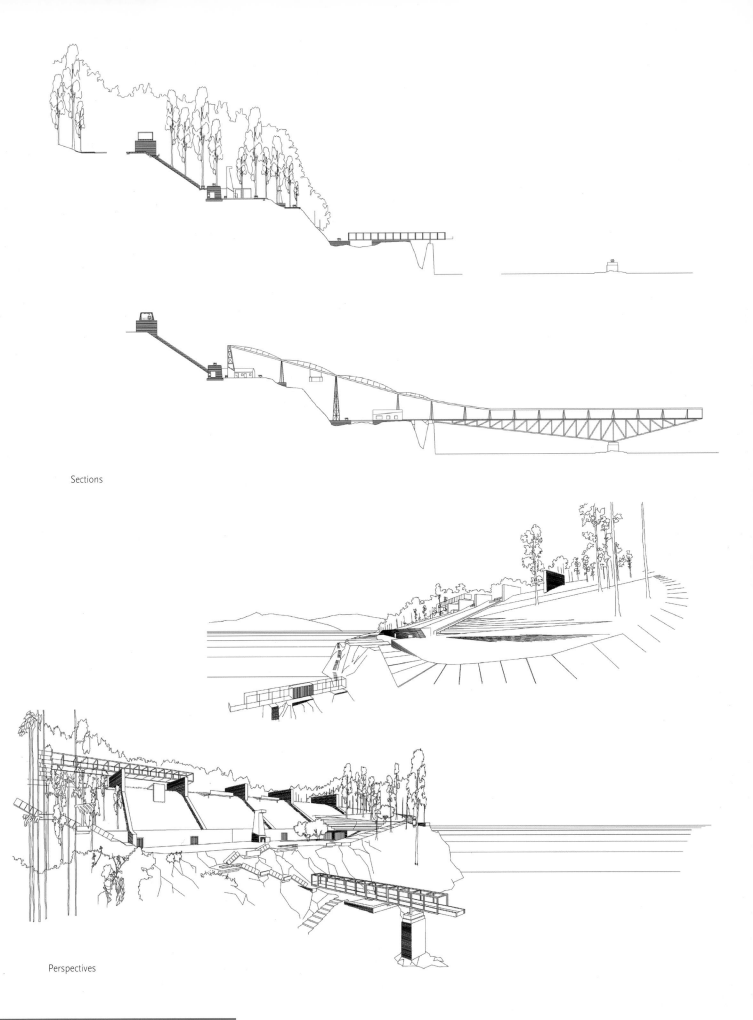

Sections

Perspectives

Urban
Spaces

Traffic Organizers

Streets

Urban Furniture

Installations

01   Traffic Junction Odenskog
Odenskog, Sweden

02   Diwang Park B
Shenzhen, China

03   Teruel Urban Development
Teruel, Spain

04   Pedestrian Area FUZI
Innichen, Italy

05   Passeig Garcia Fària
Barcelona, Spain

06   Fira Montjuïc 2 in Barcelona
Barcelona, Spain

07   Clarke Quay Redevelopment
Singapore, Singapore

08   Stadtlounge St. Gallen
Saint Gallen, Switzerland

09   Town Hall Square
Toronto, Canada

10   Bali Memorial
King's Park, Perth, Australia

11   Impluvium
Beigo Building, Montreal, Canada

12   Harmony of Opposites
Ottawa, Canada

13   Trans[plant]
Ottawa, Canada

14   In Vitro
Grand-Métis, Canada

15   Litlatún
Reykjavik, Iceland

16   Mente la-menta?
Chaumont-sur-Loire, France

17   Solange
Lyons, France

18   Amoeba 2
Martin Place, Sydney. Australia

Photo © Lennart Jonasson

Traffic Junction Odenskog

Odenskog, Sweden   2007

LANDSCAPE ARCHITECTS
GORA Art & Landscape

CLIENT
The Swedish Road Administration

PARTNERS
Monica Gora, Jens Linnet, Sara Schlyter, Mårten Setterblad (team); Benny Ersson, The Swedish Road Administration Mitt (constructors); Vägverket Produktin (general contract)

AREA
322,917 SF

COST
450,000 euros

This roundabout intersection at Odenskog is a principal entrance to the city of Östersund in the north of Sweden, about 300 miles north of Stockholm. Östersund is a major winter outdoor recreation destination, so the marking of its entrance from the highway is of great importance for its many visitors. The project is intended to help give presence to the entrance to the city from the E14 highway. The natural landscape here at the edge of the urban area of Östersund is characterized by dense coniferous forests, primarily spruce, interspersed with small-scale agriculture.

To emphasize the significance of the place, the landscape within the 460-foot-diameter circular junction has been carefully shaped with low sloping banks and planted with lines of amelamchier spicata (thicket shadbush, a flowering bush with blue colored berries and dark foliage). But the signature elements are the six light sculptures asymmetrically dispersed across the broad sloping landscape of the traffic circle.

These light sculptures, although abstract, are vaguely reminiscent of Russian onion domes or some sort of seed pod. Each is as big as a car and so relates to the scale of the passing vehicles. They flank the highway and seem on the verge of becoming animate: a welcoming committee waiting patiently. Their icy-blue-towards-turquoise color is opaque in the daylight but semitransparent when lit from within at night. This effect is obtained by the sculptural pods' construction with fiberglass reinforced polyester plastic. The color complements its surroundings in every season whether set off against the snowy white landscape of winter or the lush forest-greens of the northern summer. Illumination is always a welcome element in the far north with its long winter nights. Östersund lies just a few degrees south of the Arctic Circle.

This traffic circle with its landscape of illuminated sculptures has attracted much attention and discussion. Within a short time it has established Odenskog as a place with its own identity and as the entrance to the city of Östersund.

Waiting by the side of the highway, the illuminated pod sculptures
distinguish this junction that serves as the principal entry to Östersund
from the highway. Their blue-turquoise color is set off nicely by the snow,
reflecting the blue shade of shadows cast in the snow.

Sketch

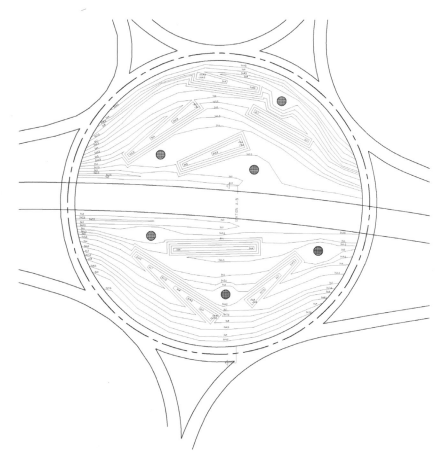

Plan

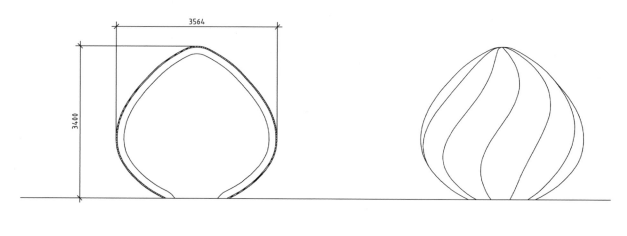

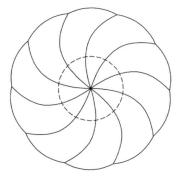

Section, Elevation and Plan

Photo © Yan Meng, Jiu Chen

Diwang Park B

Shenzhen, China   2005

LANDSCAPE ARCHITECTS
Urbanus Architecture & Design

CLIENT
City of Shenzhen

AREA
43,056 SF

The site is a typical leftover scrap of urban land that has been unfortunately ignored by the city administration. It is hemmed-in by major thoroughfares and the sun-blotting skyscrapers of the central Luohu District of Shenzhen, China, near Hong Kong and the Pearl River delta. The site is approximately triangular and fairly long and narrow. It sits at the intersection of several of Shenzhen's very busy avenues and astride a covered canal. A public restroom remains prominently positioned in the middle of the site. Another city street runs under the site as well.

The designers arrived at their ideas for the park from a bird's-eye view of the site from the adjacent Diwang Tower, the tallest structure in the city. This view revealed a kinetic scene of flowing lines, lights, and colors in a busy urban juncture. Flowing lines and flowing paths were forms that allowed the designers to accommodate the complexity or the site and its irregular shape. The flowing lines are also suggestive of the dynamic spirit of modern Shenzhen: a city in constant motion and constantly in the act of flowing. As the flows converge, split, and overlap they are constantly releasing dynamic energy, like the twining, flowing rivers of this city.

The park's design materializes this image. A series of curving linear elements are in dialog with the context of flowing traffic. This approach also allowed the designers to overcome the irregularities of the site and create the required connections. These undulating pathways enrich the pedestrian experience. Although very regular in width and finish, the designers played with these paths as if they were ribbons, bending up here and there to form seating benches or to bridge an irregularity in the landscape. An existing public restroom is sheathed in metal mesh, forming a dark and calming backdrop for the park. A regularly-spaced series of screen structures containing plantings of bamboo function as light boxes. These structures were added to provide peaceful resting areas that are sorely needed in this chaotic urban setting.

The park is set down in the middle of a chaotic and dynamical
developing urban environment. Various treatments are applied to the
flowing stripes that cover the entire park, ranging from solid brick through
a more porous surface with brick and grass to stripes that are entirely
planted in grass

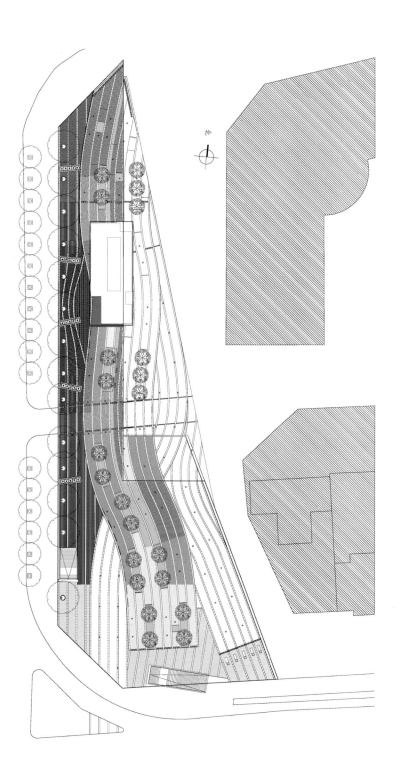

Plan

Renderings

A brick path bends up playfully to form an impromptu seat. The existing restroom building is wrapped in metal mesh, forming a dark, abstract volume. Screen structures placed at a regular rhythm sit ready to be planted with bamboo and help provide a little shelter from the urban environment

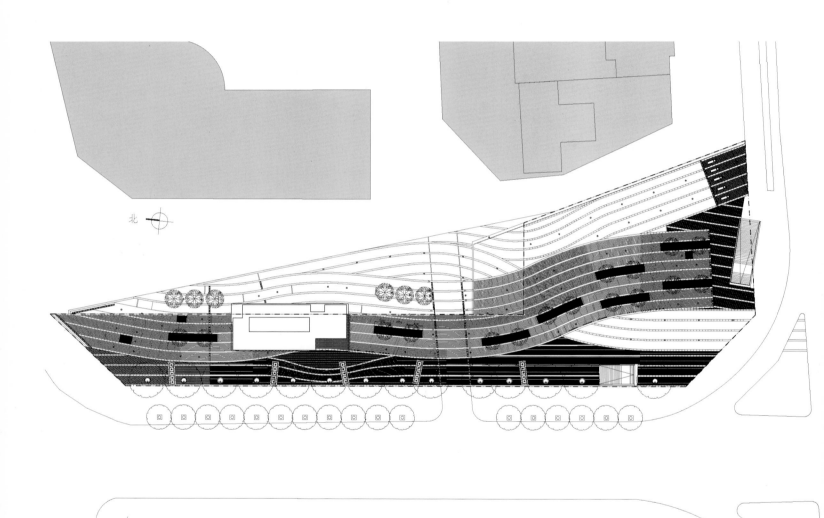

Site Plan

Photo © Hisao Suzuki

Teruel Urban Development

Teruel, Spain   2003

LANDSCAPE ARCHITECTS
David Chipperfield Architects, Fermín Vázquez/B720 Arquitectos

CLIENT
Diputación General de Aragón

PARTNERS
Obiol Moya & Asociados (structural engineer); Perfil 7 (services engineer); César Esparza (industrial engineer); Tirwal Técnica (quantity surveyor); Necso SA (general contractor)

AREA
84,712 SF

1921 was the inauguration of the monumental staircase built to resolve the actual difference in height between a street called the Paseo del Óvalo and the street on which the train station is located. The work covered by a 2001 reform to the area affects the staircase's entire surroundings. This urban renovation attempts to create a formal unity and a homogenous path from the lower level of the train station's plaza to the Glorieta area; this historical path runs above very old walls. The intervention includes reforms to the station's plaza, the construction of an elevator connecting this area to the historical structure and the renovation of the Paseo del Óvalo. For this last aspect, an attempt was made to recuperate the spirit of pedestrian passage and the peculiarity of its balcony through the creation of two parallel spaces: one destined to serve moving traffic and another, more important one, for pedestrians. Two lines of light dictate vehicular traffic, which is separated from pedestrian traffic by a double row of trees. The pedestrian area, developed on its own continuous level, also serves as an infrastructure to encourage specific activities within the city, like the Vaquilla festivals, street markets and medieval fairs. Visually, the Paseo del Óvalo is connected with the lower plaza thanks to the uniform use of paving stones.

In the station's plaza, the principal element is a white stone path that runs along an incline, leading towards a hollow rectangular space of ample dimensions. Hollowed out of the wall, the space simulates a new door to the city. In reality it's nothing more than a simple sign towards the elevators. These connect the plaza with the older structure and, on the upper level of the path, rise in the shape of translucent prisms. The plaza's new space is projected as appropriate grounds for the monumental staircase while ceding all attention to the structure.

Paving, lighting and urban fixtures adopt a formal unity that helps to
create an area for enjoyment. The path, marked by discrete elements, is
free of architectural barriers, considering that it is constructed as a solitary
and continuous level.

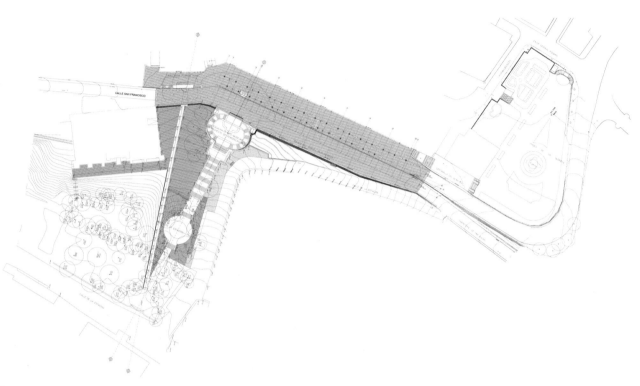

Plan

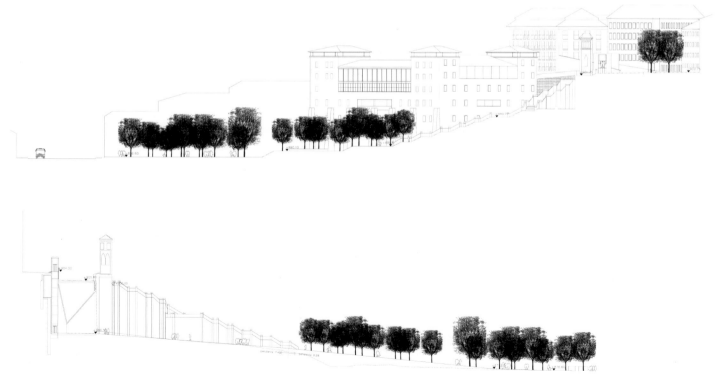

Sections

The new elevators become an alternative to the staircase that connects the older structures with the station's lower level. Located in a hollow excavated from the wall, these elevators rise up onto the path-level like glass and cement prisms

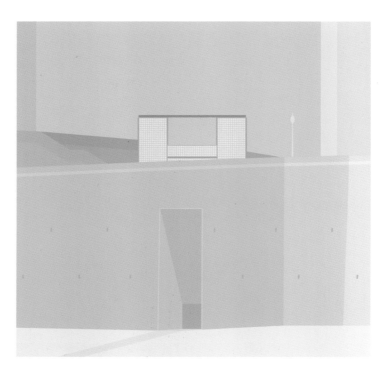

Elevation

Section

Photo © AllesWirdGut Architektur, Hertha Hurnaus

Pedestrian Area FUZI

Innichen, Italy   2002

LANDSCAPE ARCHITECTS
AllesWirdGut Architektur

CLIENT
Comune di San Candido

PARTNERS
*Sebastian Gretzer, Gilles Delalex (team);
Baubüro Bruneck, Peter Hofer (assistance);
Sulzerbacher Walter (structural); P. I. Zanotto
Franco (electrical engineering); Konzept Licht
Steindl (lighting consulting)*

AREA
38,750 SF

COST
570,000 euros

Innichen is a small transalpine locality in the mountainous foothills of the Dolomites, on the Austrian border with Italy. Because of its public infrastructure it is the economic and social heart of Hochpuster Valley. The important role tourism plays in its development is reflected in the fact that it has more hotel beds than inhabitants. It was born as an intersection uniting the diverse routes and bridges over which people and goods traveled, and, to this day, that intersection remains the center of the city. Much like other tourist destinations, municipal authorities decided to do away with traffic in the center to convert the streets and squares into open public spaces.

This generous redesign employed contemporary intervention techniques to return the urban center to an appearance similar to what it had before the invasion of cars. For this, a homogenous integration was sought, cautious and extremely respectful of the surroundings: many autochthonous materials were used from local quarries. The dark green tones mimic those of the nearby forest of conifer trees and the pebbled pavement matches the gray mountains while evoking the historic paths that started the city.

This aesthetic sensibility is complemented by a functional design that adapts to the pronounced seasonal changes characteristic of life in Innichen: overcrowded in summer and winter, empty in spring and fall. Keeping this in mind, and thanks to ingenious regulations, the usable surface can be amplified or reduced at will. During calmer seasons, various clearly defined spaces are filled with water to make small geometric lakes, while other spaces are substituted with robust flowers. This control of spatial density has aesthetic, social and psychological components that positively influence the city's cycles and its inhabitants.

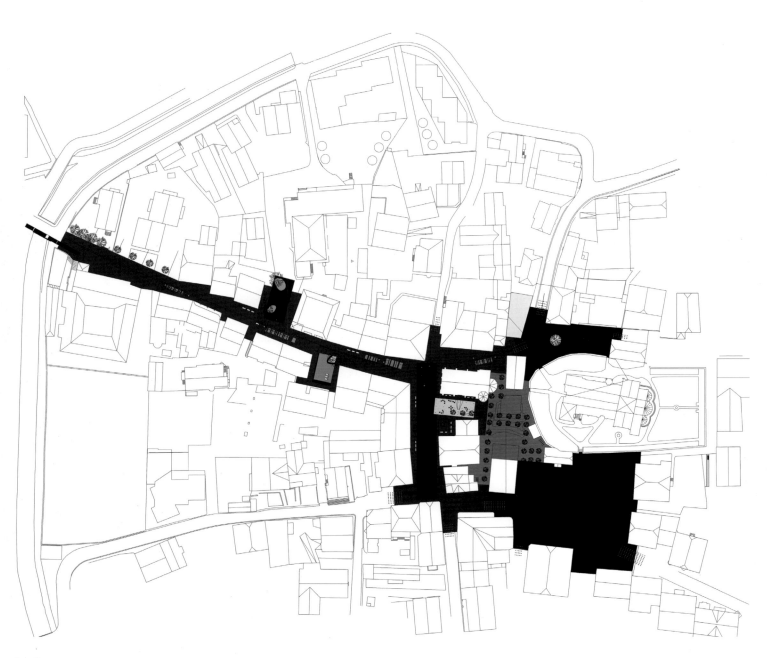

Fleeing from trite and inefficient prescriptions for the conversion of urba[n]
centers, the design for the intervention in Innichen gives real solutions the[y]
adapt to the intense seasonal fluctuations suffered by the city. Th[e]
architects opted to create a functional project that permits bicycle parkin[g]
via the amplification and reduction of usable surfac[e]

Site Plan

The succession of different platforms creates diverse atmospheres an
distributes the space into areas for intense activity or rest an
contemplation, like the pond. Night lighting is characterized by the use c
green tones that mimic the surrounding vegetation

Conceptual Drawing

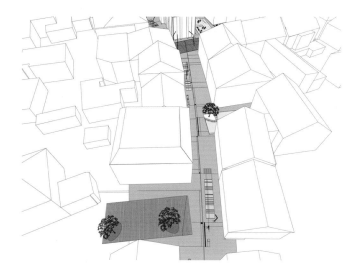

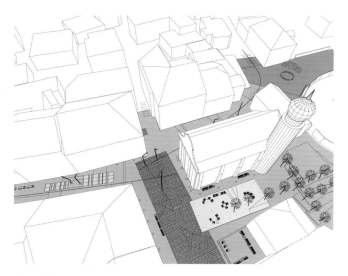

Perspectives

Photo © Roger Casas

Passeig Garcia Fària

Barcelona, Spain   2004

LANDSCAPE ARCHITECTS
Ravetllat & Ribas Arquitectes

CLIENT
Infrastructures del Levant de Barcelona SA

PARTNERS
Pere Joan Ravetllat, Carme Ribas (authors); COMSA (contractor); RIAZU (construction management); Gecsa, Esteyco, Mireia Fernández, Mireia Rubio, Anna Zahonero (consultants)

AREA
529,660 SF

COST
4,800,000 euros

This intervention presented very particular characteristics that elevated its level of difficulty: the intersection of Selva de Mar Street and Josep Pla Street, the impossibility of landscaping the roof of an underground parking garage and the difficulty of a space less than a mile long by only 131 feet wide. The adopted solution accentuates the dimensions of the clearing made by the parking garage roof through the use of two different colored asphalts. This strip, laid out for the visitor's enjoyment, has been provided with areas for fitness, jogging, cycling and other leisure activities. The area that allowed for landscaping has been covered with green trapezoidal pieces that fit with the parking garage roof through the use of flowerbeds and elevated platforms that suggest balconies facing the sea.

The presence of parking ramps established a new difficulty in planning, considering that these were situated far from the roadway.

The problem was resolved with vegetation that tempers the effect of these mammoth entryways. For drainage, an incline towards Garcia Fària Street was made in the transverse section, while also increasing the gradient of the parking lot.

The vegetation chosen was conditioned by the singularity of the surroundings, which is close to the sea: organized in strips, the flowerbeds on the Garcia Fària Street side hold shrubbery of differing heights, while the double-sided flowerbeds are covered with grass on one side, and white oleander on the other. Palm and other ornamental trees are placed along the path in groups of two or three; these are also present in the linear flowerbed that borders the road. High street-lamps illuminate both sides of the avenue and help to conserve, at all times, a uniform height, independent of the geographical point on which they are installed.

*The distinct topography called for a small increase in the gradient slope of
the path. The paved asphalt, of two different colors, marks the pedestrian
path, located above the highway and a parking garage. Along the length
of the structure, a series of activity areas were constructed for public
leisure.*

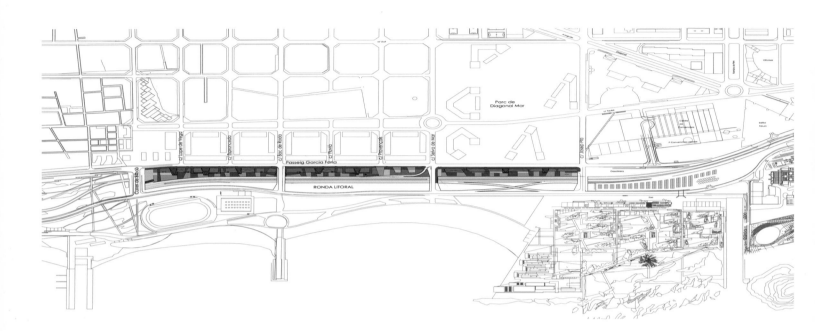

Site Plan

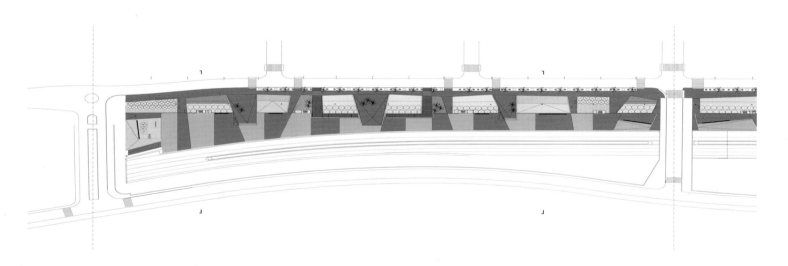

Plan

The proximity of the sea determined the choice of certain types of
vegetation: the flowerbeds are planted with grass and shrubbery in strips
parallel to the pathway. The new road layout determines a modification in
circulation that directs all traffic towards the road north of the pathway.

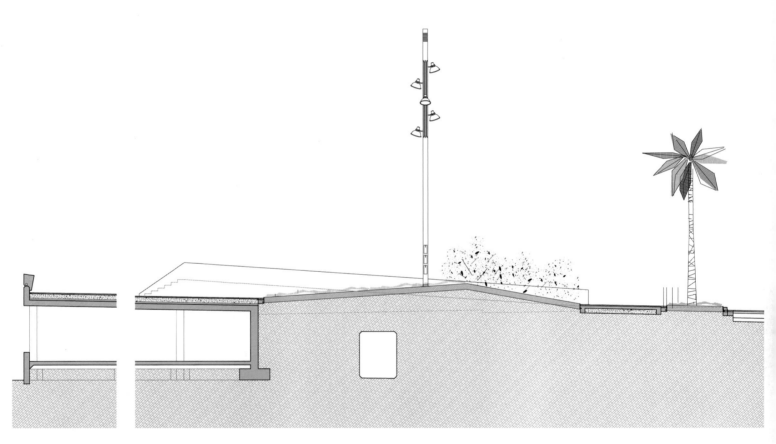

Section

Photo © Stéphane Llorca

Fira Montjuïc 2 in Barcelona

Barcelona, Spain   2005

LANDSCAPE ARCHITECTS
Toyo Ito & Architects Associates, JML Arquitectura del Agua

CLIENT
Ajuntament de Barcelona

PARTNERS
Stéphane Llorca, Nicolas Llense (consultants); IDOM (engineering)

AREA
72,118 SF

As happens with many peripheral areas that had a very industrial profile in the past, today the Barcelona Fairgrounds, an old suburban area, has been incorporated into the urban fabric as a the result of an ambitious plan of transformation and rehabilitation. An integral part of it, the Montjuïc Fairgrounds 2, was recently the subject of an international contest to design its expansion. The winning project consisted of a new complex of pavilions and was designed by Japanese architect Toyo Ito. The nature of the location–its function as an important center of lines of communication and transport–and that derived of its future uses–an infrastructure destined to hold a wide diversity of fairground programming–determined the project's conception as a new gateway to Barcelona, a new urban access of the highest magnitude. Special emphasis was placed on interconnecting the entrances to the different pavilions, which were configured as huge curved atriums or small squares that

would communicate between themselves. Following the directives given by the Japanese architect, the studio called JML Arquitectura del Agua (Architecture of Water) was given charge of developing the different concepts for water treatment; water being an omnipresent element in the 72,118 square foot surface of the fairgrounds. Various groups of fountains delineate this layout of small squares and distribute the space by separating pedestrian areas from those destined for traffic. Its spouted streams create studied volumes of water that jet out between benches with lines that match these. In their rise and fall, the jets of water draw smooth arcs that mimic and highlight the architectural complex's geometry. Its design has been tweaked to achieve that clean and curved effect, very purified, that lends the area an impression of character and originality.

For the sqares that surround the pavilions, the architectural studio decide
to develop some of the concepts belonging to architect Toyo Ito. Water
an omnipresent element in the design of this space: the jets were designe
so that they would reflect the geometry of this architectural complex. Th
smooth arcs that these describe emphasize the project's urban gatewa
characte

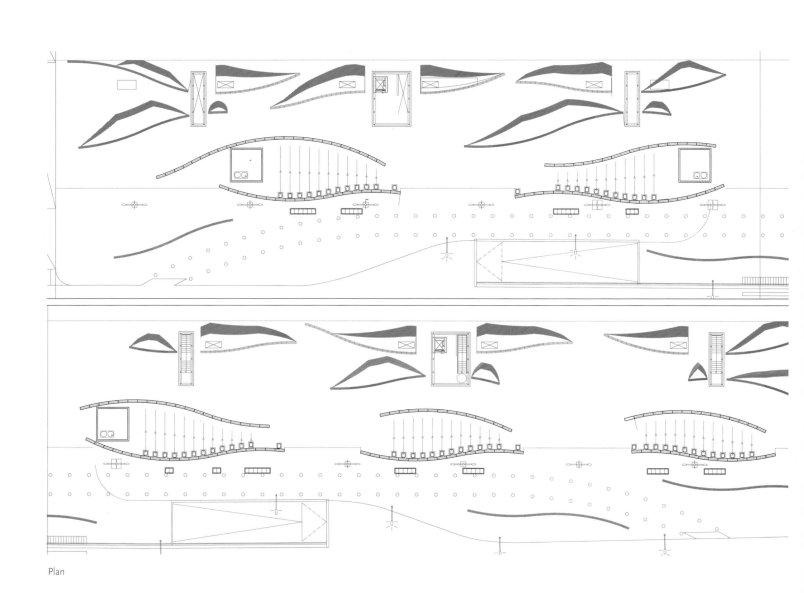

Plan

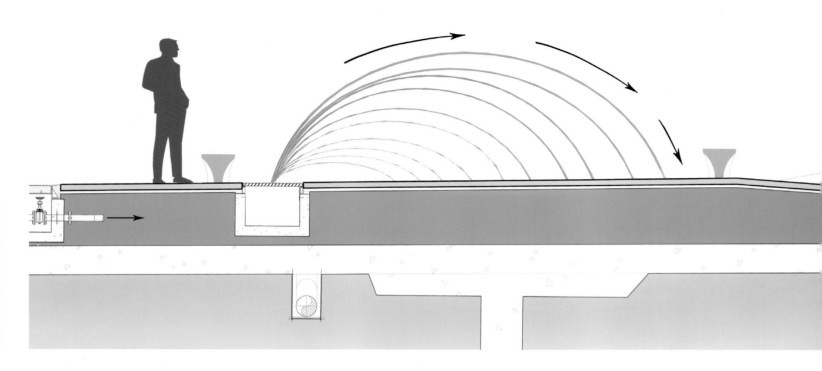

Sketch

Photo © Jeremy San

Clarke Quay Redevelopment

Singapore, Singapore   2006

LANDSCAPE ARCHITECTS
SMC Alsop

CLIENT
Capitaland Commercial Ltd

PARTNERS
Stephen Pimbley, Peter Sim, Jan Felix Clostermann, Gyn Kong, Tan Ming Yin, Torrance Goh, Sophia David, Chin Kean Kok, Sven Steiner (team); RSP (engineering); Tensys, Atelier One (structural engineering); ARUP (development); Kajima (contractor)

AREA
7.4 acres

COST
42,493,600 euros

The motive behind the renovation of the historic waterfront along the Singapore River resided in the necessity of bringing both tourist and citizen presence to this part of the city. Clarke Quay is characterized by the architecture of its old warehouses, situated in front of the river. In the last twenty years, the area witnessed different renovations, the 19th century buildings have been renovated and the area evolved into a neighborhood of stores, restaurants and places of entertainment. This last project is part of a subsequent modernization of the riverfront, which was to be transformed into a strolling path and an area for exclusive restaurants.

A terrace was built facing the sea to recuperate more space and separate the path from the table area. Here a series of platforms was installed, covered with umbrellas called bluebells, which protect the patrons from the sun and rain. Lit at night by a large variety of colors, these umbrellas are reflected in the river's water and recall the lighting effect suggested by traditional Chinese lanterns.

The series of umbrellas are connected to a larger system of shelters that cover the neighborhood's four main arteries, which are converted into galleries of a more contemporary stripe where one can go shopping or for a walk thanks to this agreeable micro-climate.

The covering has been devised to protect the visitors from the city's extreme climate: rainfall, humidity and high temperatures. The structure is formed by huge Teflon umbrellas supported by a metallic pillar that cover the rooftops of the buildings. While these umbrellas provide shade and cover, a breeze is made by fans built into their supporting metallic structure. The trees planted along the street add a beneficial climate to the surroundings, much like the way a fountain underlines a feeling of freshness. The lighting system within these covered streets is based on the use of different colors, daring and changeable, and the use of spotlights built into the ground.

Transformed into a neighborhood of restaurants and exclusive bars, the old
Singapore River waterfront has been dotted with a protective system
against the heat and rain: giant umbrellas regulate the temperature
within this covered area.

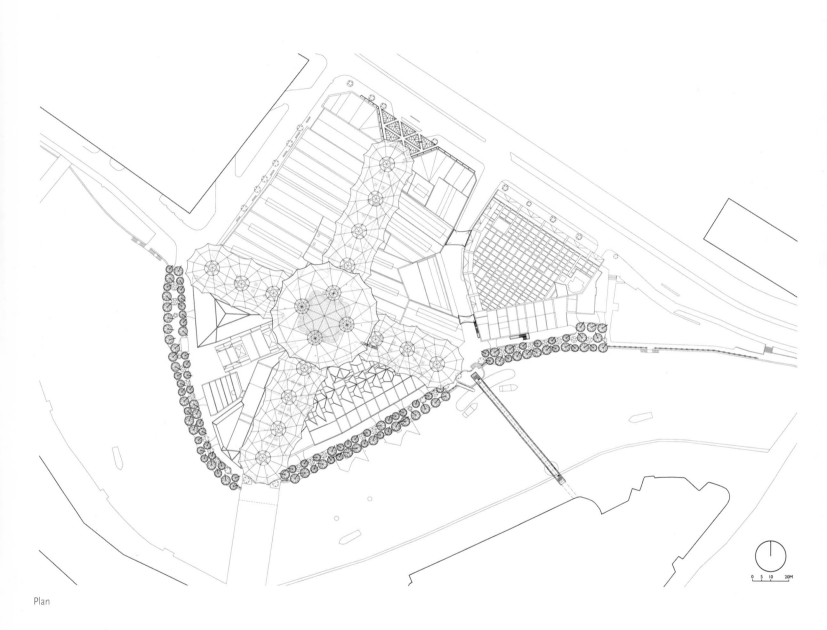

Plan

3D Model

Photo © Hannes Thalmann, Marc Wetli

Stadtlounge St. Gallen

St. Gallen, Switzerland   2005

LANDSCAPE ARCHITECTS
Carlos Martínez Architekten, Pipilotti Rist/Hauser & Wirth

CLIENT
Schweizer Verband der Raiffeisenbanken, Stadt Saint Gallen

PARTNERS
Vogt & Partner (lightplaning)

AREA
48,438 SF

COST
1,302,500 euros

In the financial district of the Swiss city of St. Gallen this breakthrough design in public space is found. Architect Carlos Martínez and the Swiss artist Pipilotti Rist have transformed a monotonous intersection into an urban lounge characterized by soft pavement made of rubber and colored an intense red. The main idea was to create a carpet that would extend over the entire surface, cover the fixtures and give the impression that these come up from the ground. The benches, tables and chairs adapt to the material and offer the users the possibility of touching it easily by bringing it closer to them. Its agreeable texture contrasts with the bustle and coldness of any office area and converts a space into an elegant public lounge that plays with the concepts of interior and exterior.

The carpet extends to the edge of the buildings. The relation between interior and exterior seems inverted since the building facades can be interpreted as lounge walls. Few plants were used and only four tall gingkos, elected especially for the chromatic change of their leaves and their contrast with the red material, were used. Lighting is based on huge bubble-shaped lamps suspended from steel cables that seem to float like sculptures. These elements provide a level of contrast with the uniformity of the pavement and bathe the entire area with a scenic light. In fact, the lounge offers different lighting possibilities in accord with the time of day and the seasons. The light can be adapted to accommodate different activities.

One of the project's fundamental concepts was to break with the habits of vision. The multitude of sensations the visitor experiences will inspire him to intellectually own the place and to interpret it into as many different ways as there are people. From its genesis, the project has resisted any one unique or correct interpretation. Today, this old intersection is open to the outside, inviting people to enter an urban lounge where man, and not traffic, is the center of attention.

The urban fixture elements seem to emerge from the ground and their soft
and rounded shapes contrast with the marked lines of the surrounding
buildings. The placement of these elements, accompanied by the intensity
of the lights, creates a meditative and comfortable atmosphere in
apparently adverse surroundings

Site Plan

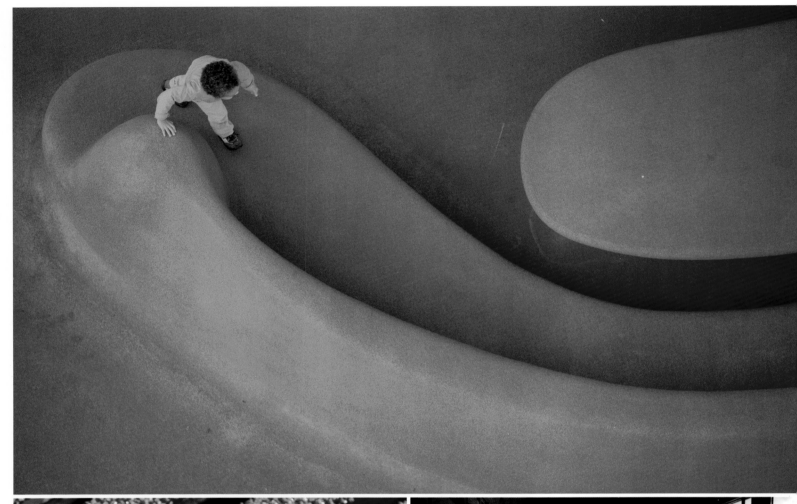

The intense red paving covers the entire space like a carpet and eliminate
traditional concepts like street, square, sidewalk, etcetera. It proposes
complete redefinition of public space. The lighting changes according to
the time of day and the various activities involved

Photo © Neil Fox

Town Hall Square

Toronto, Canada   2005

LANDSCAPE ARCHITECTS
Janet Rosenberg & Associates

CLIENT
Great Gulf Group of Companies

PARTNERS
*Jean-Pierre Morin (artist); Tucker Highrise,
Vander Busche Irrigation (consultants);
Aldershot Landscape Contractors Ltd (general
contractor)*

AREA
0.62 acres

COST
644,400 euros

Right in the middle of Toronto, in the neighborhood of Yorkville, the construction of a new public space paralleled the construction of a 36 floor apartment building. The objective was to create a pedestrian square that, aside from contributing to a rise in green areas, would enter into dialog with the space's architecture, presided over by the modern apartment building and the historic Yorkville library building. Built atop an underground parking garage, the park had to follow these directives: accommodate private and public paths, create an entrance to the parking lot and establish connections between the locale's history and its placement beside the library. Also, it had to be aesthetically attractive, from ground level and from the apartments above.

Town Hall Square is an elegant public space with daring geometry and simple patterns in the pavement and plantation that connects with its surroundings. A rich variety of green plants, including vinca, boxwood and ginkgo. give the space different textures. In huge concrete flowerpots, round boxwoods were planted that give the location rhythm. The wooden benches and the concrete discs that function as basins for the gingkos, are laid out all around and offer abundant seating. The park has an automatic sprinkler system that is regulated in conjunction with the amount of precipitation that has fallen. The gingkos and other plants were chosen specifically for their high capacity of adaptation to urban conditions.

The entryways to the adjacent buildings are differentiated from the rest of the pavement by their colors and, together with the gingkos and the benches lend the entire complex a formal sense. The lighting design provides a sophisticated ambiance and highlights elements like the 25 foot-high sculptural piece by Canadian artist Jean-Pierre Morin. This work of art attracts people while creating an interesting perspective of the whole area. The design elements make the park a functional place that absorbs the pedestrian traffic in the area and can also accommodate open-air activities and others that are library-related.

The park's design on one sole level eliminates the need for architectural
barriers and creates a visually amplified space. The concrete discs holding
the trees, aside from protecting their trunks, offer original seating. The
huge concrete flowerpots over planted surfaces offer singularity while the
colors of the pavement indicate the entryways to the adjacent buildings.

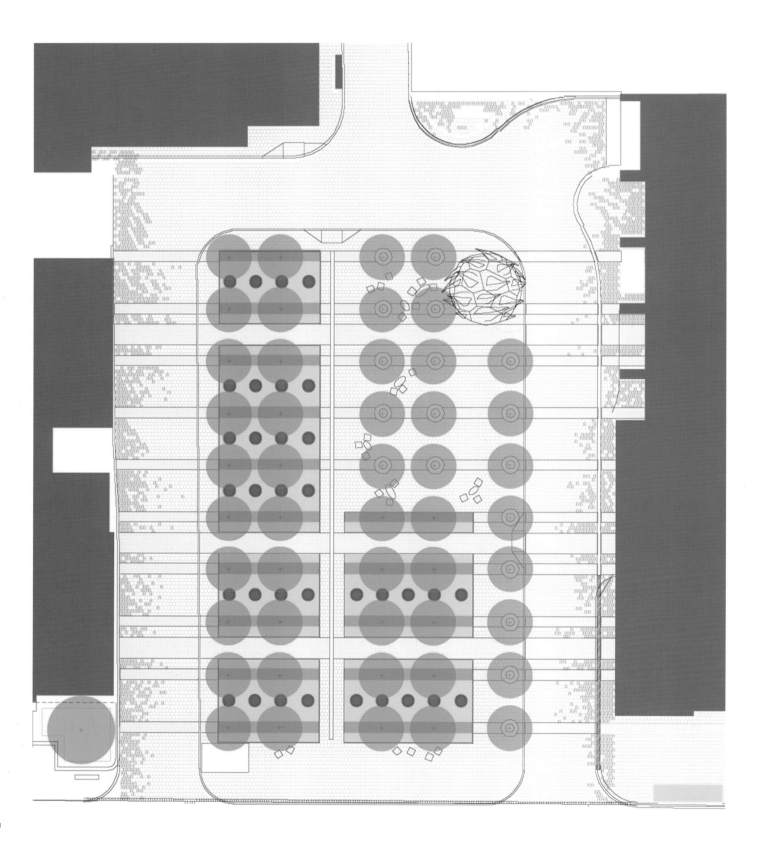

Plan

Photo © Martin Farquharson

Bali Memorial

King's Park, Perth, Australia   2003

LANDSCAPE ARCHITECTS
Donaldson & Warm Architects

CLIENT
The Department of Premier and Cabinet, The Botanic Gardens and Parks Authority

PARTNERS
Geoff Warn (design director); Simon Pendal, Tom Griffiths, David Jones (project team); Kevin Draper, Sally Morgan (artists); David Smith, Plan E (landscape architects); Brian Nelson, Capital House Australasia, Guy Tomlinson, CCD Australia, Saissay Degeffa (engineering); Mark Spry, Stuart Sadgrove, John Holland Pty Ltd (contractors)

AREA
1 acre (King's Park)

COST
409,400 euros

The Bali Memorial was born in 2007 to remember the victims of a terrorist attempt that occurred on October the 12th in 2002. Conceived as a place for remembrance, reflection and community, the monument stands in Kings Park, a green area to the west of Perth with views of the city and Swan River. The location was chosen by the families of the victims.

Structured around natural elements like water and light, the memorial monument is developed around two axes: one opens on views of the estuary, while the other is directed towards a specific point on the horizon where, each dawn on October 12th, a ray of sunlight illuminates the commemorative plaque. The fence forms a type of portal through which the sunlight is channeled for this suggestive effect. The memorial's design is the result of an analysis and synthesis of the typology of Australian suburban residential areas to give the victim's relatives a sense of familiarity.

The garden of remembrance was made with sandstone, granite and steel. The memorial's pertinence with the culture and the local landscape is demonstrated in the series of images depicting native flora and fauna found on the steel walls. Texts and artwork by local artists are engraved into the walls and floor. A rest area with tables and benches is protected by a fence and a shelter that is differentiated from the other walls by its wood dressing.

The Bali Memorial is conceived as a meeting point and a place for reflection on the terrorist attacks that occurred on the 12th of October in 2002. Encouraged by authorities, the memorial was built in a location chosen by the victims' families.

Plan

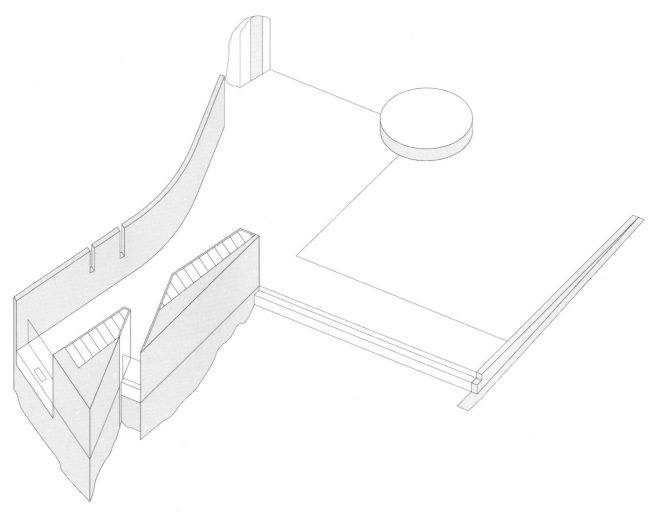

Bali Memorial Axonometric

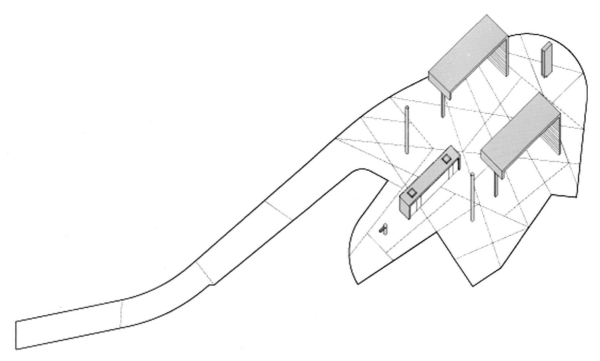

Picnic Area Axonometric

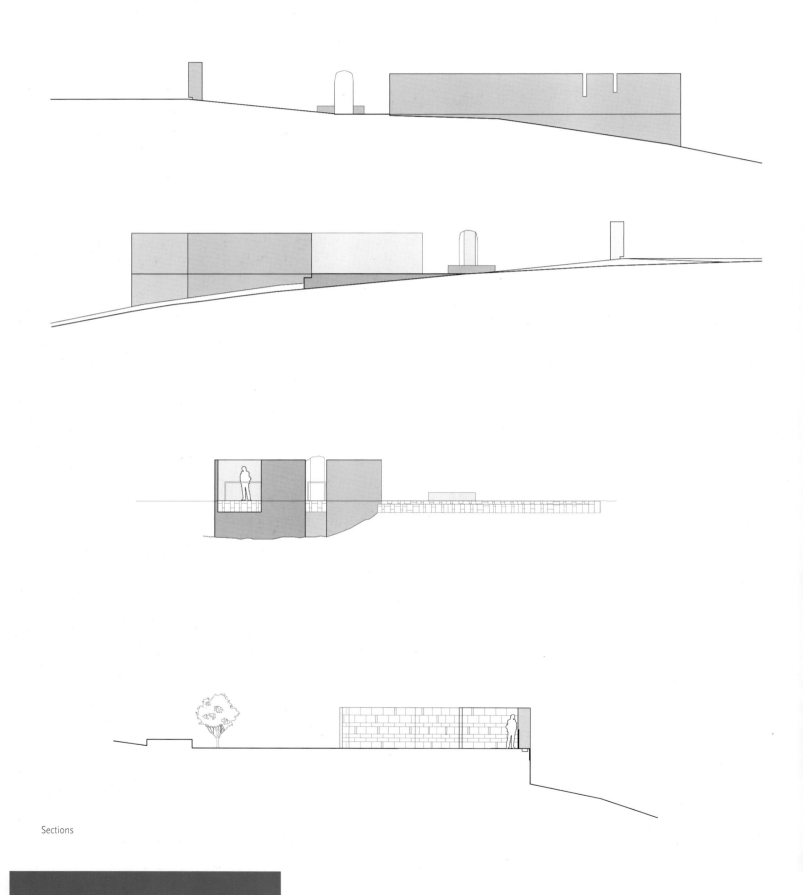

Sections

Photo © NIP Paysage

Impluvium

Belgo Building, Montreal, Canada   2004

LANDSCAPE ARCHITECTS
NIP Paysage

CLIENT
La Biennale de Montréal, Monopole Galerie d'Architecture, Conseil des Arts et Lettres du Québec

AREA
32,292 SF

COST
13,400 euros

Like the fleeting traces of a rainfall, the concentric circles of blue are immortalized in the roof of a building situated in the center of Montreal, Canada. Impluvium is the name of the installation made by NIP Paysage to celebrate the Biennial Exhibition of Montreal in the fall of 2004.

In the architecture of ancient Rome, the impluvium was a pool situated in the central patio, where rain water channeled from the roof was collected. With this idea in mind, the young Canadian landscapers have intervened in the 32,292-square-foot roof of the Belgo building as if it were a pool. Using the horizontal structure like a board, the landscapers have composed an urban scale scenario, giving cause for reflection upon the enormous potential contained in the thousands of building rooftops available. The last frontier of urban adjustment, the rooftop represents a forgotten territory, virgin and potentially available for transformation

through a multitude of solutions beyond contemplating the use of vegetation. The gray color which impregnates and dominates the city rooftops can be interrupted, and perhaps completely defeated, by a multiplicity of frescoes and different installations of various colors. These can achieve a radical transformation in the image and skyline of a metropolis.

The installation, as simple as it is severe, is nothing more than three different shades of blue paint on the black asphalt of the flat roof: gigantic, intercepting concentric circles that only the exterior borders of the roof are able to stop from spreading further. This urban-scale liquid board takes in and reproduces the rain drops that fall, one after the other, on the rooftops of Montreal, enlarging them. Visible only from a higher elevation, the work, simple and efficient in its message, also reminds that above the city nature continues to exist.

Only visible from a higher elevation, this installation on the roof of a
Montreal building suggests a reflection on the evaluation of these
unexploited surfaces, which can transform the perspective of a city

Plan

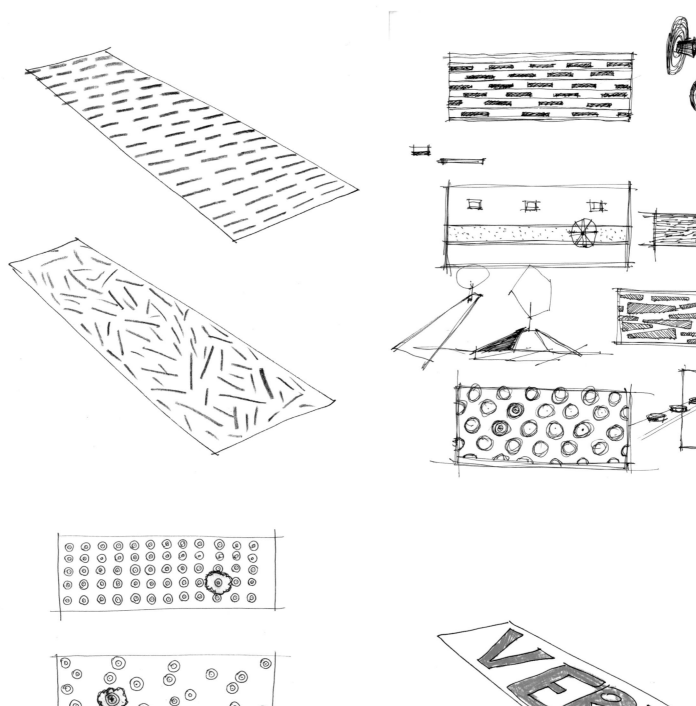

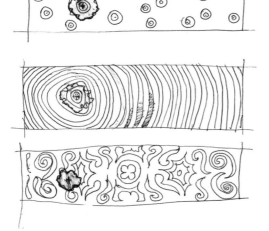

Conceptual Sketches

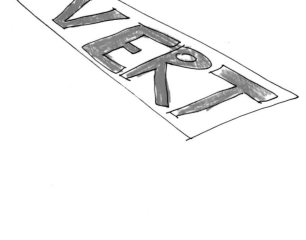

Conceptual Sketch

Photo © Johnathan Hayward

Harmony of Opposites

Ottawa, Canada   2002

LANDSCAPE ARCHITECTS
Janet Rosenberg & Associates

CLIENT
Canadian Tulip Festival

PARTNERS
Art Metal Works (constructor); Oriole Landscaping Ltd (general contractor)

AREA
194 SF

COST
13,600 euros

Harmony of Opposites was born in honor of the Canadian Tulip Festival organized in 2001 in Ottawa. Open to the public for only 18 days in May, the creation had to use live flowers and frame them in a spectacular setting. The stars of the installation, tulips serve as a pretext for deeper reflection about the relation between art and the landscape.

The installation, created by landscapers Janet Rosenberg & Associates is undoubtedly inspired by Holland. It's not only a tribute to the masters of the countryside and principle source of economy but an homage to modern artists: the works of Mondrian and those of Claes Oldenburg and Coosje van Bruggen, with their colors and harmonious shapes, inspire the landscapers and become a model for an imaginative relation between art and nature. Paradoxically, Mondrian's rejection of nature led the project team to unite the formal sobriety of abstract art with the vitality of flowers. The installation fuses different rectangular patches of tulips delimited by black borders beside a blue plexiglass cube, that give shape to a three-dimensional version of the Dutch painter's work. The references to Oldenburg and van Bruggen are found in the four metallic structures erected above the tulip flowerbed. A complete interpretation of the piece is found in the contrast between the lack of organicity in the paintings of Mondrian and the nature of the tulips, even if they are metallic bulbs.

The installation belongs within the framework of landscape design, an art form that uses landscapes as a fundamental medium for artistic expression. The approximation of this discipline on the part of the authors is not conventional and is voluntarily taken to the extreme in order to demonstrate the ability and potential of the landscape designer.

This landscape design installation, like a painting by Mondrian, prepares a
flowerbed of rectangular patches of colored tulips, separated by black
borders. In the center of this geometric composition, four huge metallic
bulbs have been erected.

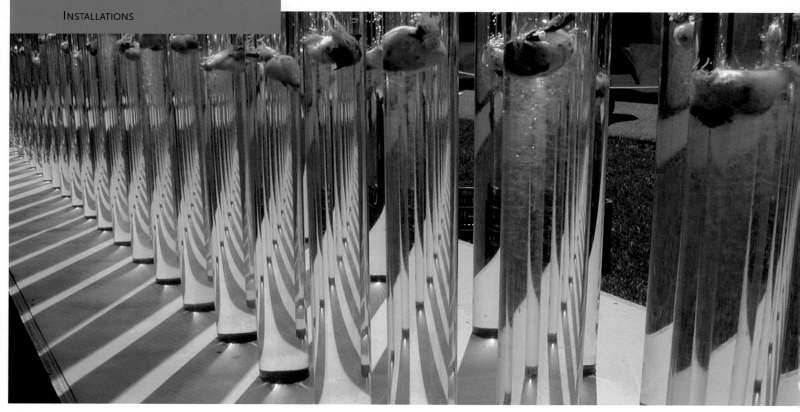

Photo © NIP Paysage

Trans[plant]

Ottawa, Canada   2002

LANDSCAPE ARCHITECTS
NIP Paysage

CLIENT
Canadian Tulip Festival

AREA
323 SF

COST
13,600 euros

The five professionals that make up NIP Paysage form part of the new wave of landscape architects that in recent years has been able to break into the international scene. Supporters of a more optimistic focus based on creativity and the use of color, these Canadian project architects believe in the transformation of external contemporary spaces through projects that range from the smallest to the largest scale. An important dose of sensibility marks all their creations, highlighted by a peculiar expressiveness that transcends functional aspects. Fascinated above all by everyday-type places often subjected to violent or constant mutations, these architects are attracted to the environmental imbalance in these places, where opportunities for expression and the creation of new landscapes can be found.

During the Canadian Tulip Festival in Ottawa, NIP Paysage exhibits a temporary installation composed of a long, thin orange strip from which rise, as if born of it, rows of white tulips. In the recesses hollowed out of the support, rows of plastic tubes are visible. Within these, tulips and other diverse bulbs float in a transparent gel. As if it were a mirror, the strip metaphorically transports a field of countryside from the flower's native home, Holland, and synthesizes its regular and ordered geometry. The 98-foot-long platform, painted a bright orange, symbolizes the color of dutch royalty's blood. At night, illumination is provided at the base of the plastic tubes to offer stage-setting effects. The installation pays homage to bulbous flowers and highlights their strong aesthetic value.

The optimistic and dynamic focus these architects display is demonstrated
by a simple but strong gesture of aesthetic impact: a long orange-colored
strip contains an exposition of white tulips. The plastic tubes hold the
tulips and bulbs that evoke the flower's country of origin, Holland.

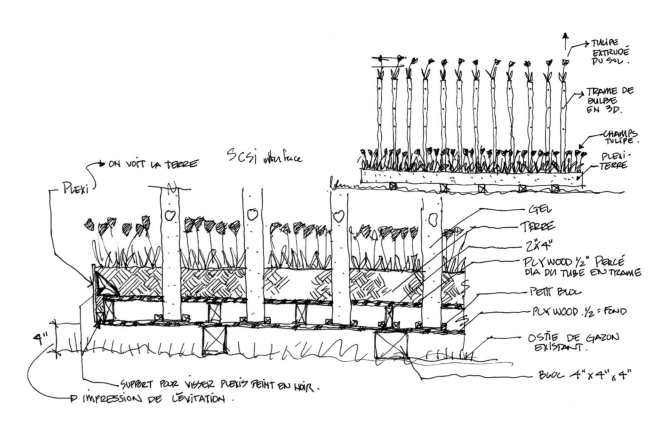

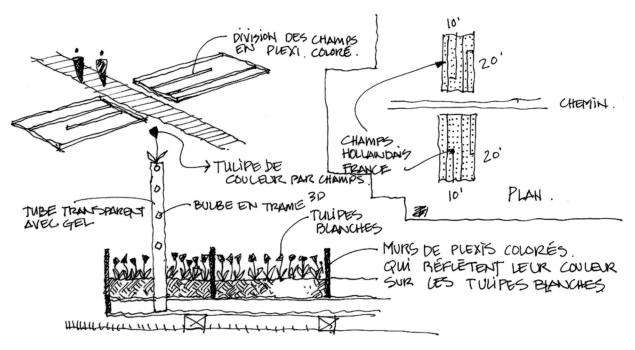

Sketches

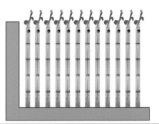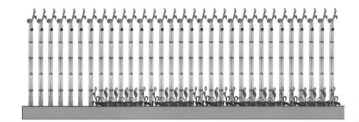

Elevations

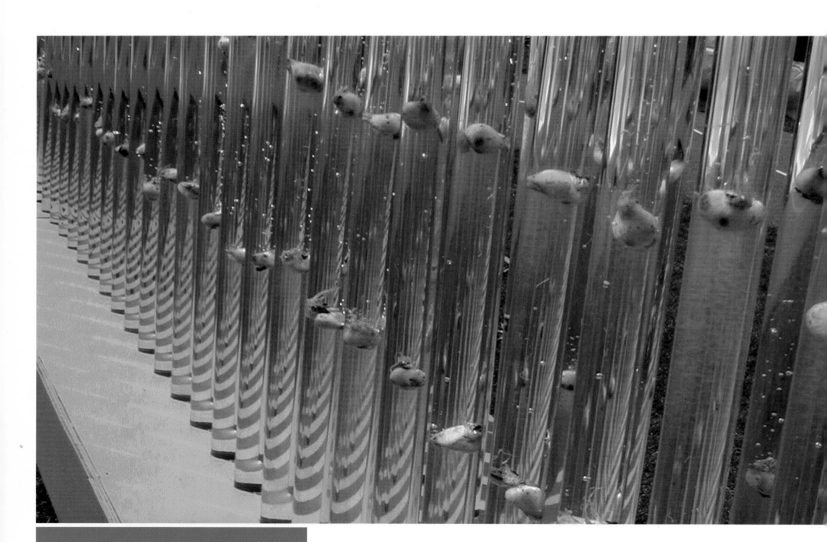

Photo © NIP Paysage, Michèle Laverdière

In Vitro

Grand-Métis, Canada   2001

LANDSCAPE ARCHITECTS
NIP Paysage

CLIENT
International Garden Festival, Reford Gardens

AREA
6,458 SF

COST
13,600 euros

Since 2000, the year of its inauguration, the International Garden Festival of Métis, in Quebec, has become a mandatory stop for landscapers. A forum for experimentation and a launching platform for new professionals, this artistic manifestation receives a multitude of tourists each year, attracted by the ephemeral installations where landscaping, architecture, design, visual arts and nature are melded to interact with each other. The In Vitro installation was presented in the festival's second edition, in 2001. It's an interpretation of Canada's jungle, reconstructed through a poetic vision of nature's wildness.

The recreational manner of interpreting each theme, reflections of the five intervening landscapers, is expressed through the use of common daily objects. Dozens of glass jars for preserves are hung with methodical delineation from a metallic structure to form a translucent wall. Inside these enigmatic jars, instead of preserves, small sprouts of white pine and pinecones float inside a col-

ored liquid. A linear wooden path is pierced with streaks of blue plastic shavings from which rise the metallic frames that support the colorful glass jars. Around them, the floor's opaque and spongy texture recalls the flooring on sports courts while also calling to mind the charred ground common to forest fires. The magic of ancestral Nordic forests is enclosed in containers that, thanks to sunlight, emit peculiar luminary effects.

This surreal atmosphere is inspired on the complexity of today's wildlife system, which in addition to being a cultural reference is a place for contemporary industrial production and exploitation. The debate over the jungle, generated here in a recreational manner by these landscapers, provokes an aesthetic pleasure in the visitor that doubles as ethical contemplation: are contemporary jungles not the victims of transformation at the hands of man, who uses them as laboratories, factories, museums and recreational areas?

Inside the translucent panels, composed of glass jars, In Vitro synthesizes the significance of today's jungles. It's a poetic labor that at the same time takes the visitor to a marvelous place of ethical contemplation. Metaphorically, the magic of Nordic forests is enclosed inside containers that emit colorful luminary effects.

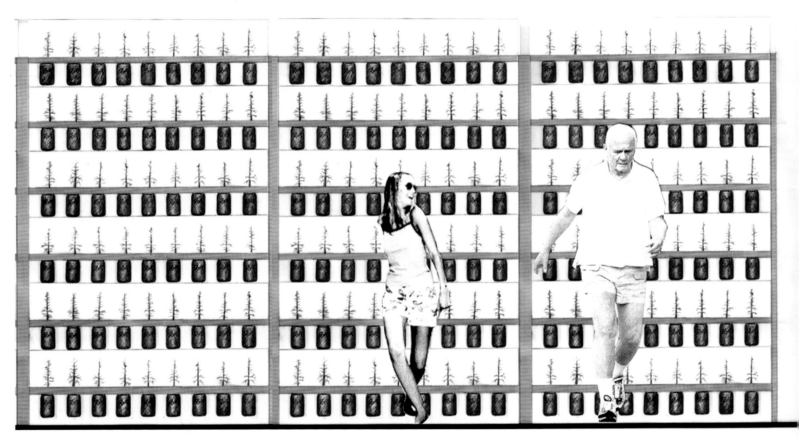

Elevation

Photo © Dagný Bjarnadóttir, Simon Schmid, Friorik Tryggvason, Brynjólfur Jónsson

Litlatún

Reykjavik, Iceland   2007

LANDSCAPE ARCHITECTS
Landslag ehf Landslagsarkitektar FÍLA

CLIENT
Magma/Kvika, Straumur Buroarás Investment Bank

PARTNERS
Túnpökuvinnslan ehf (installation); Logoflex ehf (furniture); Sindra stál hf (steel); Horticultural Department of the City of Reykjavík (maintenance)

AREA
9,192 SF

A diverse set of installations was organized for the *Magma/Kvik* exposition, held by the Reykjavik Art Museum between May and September of 2007, centered on contemporary Icelandic design. Among these was Litlatún. Located on the museum's southern patio, the work owes its name to the park that surrounds the institution, Miklatún, which means large meadow, and proposes a smaller version of this. In fact, the project connecting the museum with the park, designed in 1965, was never realized, so that space is now a gravel-covered intermediate area.

The installation proposes itself to be one option for filling this empty space through an abstract exercise that connects the park with the museum. Litlatún attempts to become an extension of the meadow, an incursion of nature and green in the gray surroundings of the building. The project is composed around three key elements. The first is the colonization of the gravel surface, thanks to the extensive introduction of green

carpeting composed of grass fibers. Like a layer of fabric, the grass is presented like a chess board, where patches are alternated with their opposite, in which the grass faces the ground. This green carpet reaches from the park to the foot of the building, creating a sensation of visual continuity. The surface is interrupted by a path of red volcanic rock that connects the park with the patio.

The second key element is comprised of yellow flags located on the eastern part of the patio. It's an undulating wall, marking a border on one side while the other side points to the statue of the Icelandic poet Einar Benediktsson erected with the construction of the park in 1965. The yellow flags reflect the gold-colored buttons that sprout from the park's grass. Lastly, the transparent fiberglass fixtures arranged around the café terrace represents a greenhouse for local vegetation. During the winter, the vegetation is substituted with lamps.

The transparent fiberglass fixtures replicate small greenhouses and comply with a dual function, containing local vegetation and serving as tables and chairs for the museum's cafeteria. Depending on the season or its use, the furniture can be opened so that the plants may be substituted by illuminating lamps, especially in the winter.

Axonometric

3D Rendering

3D Rendering

Model

Photo © Roberto Capecci, Raffaella Sini

Mente la-menta?

Chaumont-sur-Loire, France   2000

LANDSCAPE ARCHITECTS
LAND-I Archicolture

CLIENT
Conservatoire International des Parcs et Jardins et du Paysage

PARTNERS
Marco Antonini, Gianna Attiani, Roberto Capecci, Daniela Mongini, Raffaella Sini (design team)

AREA
2,691 SF

COST
25,000 euros

The International Festival of Gardens organized by the International Conservatory of Parks and Gardens and Landscaping in Chaumont-sur-Loire is a platform for contemporary garden design. Each year, more than thirty landscapers from all over the world give life to their creations on the land surrounding the castle. "Mente la-menta?" (Literal translation: Does Mint Lie?) was presented at the ninth edition of the festival in the year 2000. The absence of a slogan left the designers free to propose a personal view on the new millennium, which started in that very year. The title of the work is a play of words that may be interpreted in two different ways: Does mint lie? Can we always trust in nature to thwart the constant predatory behavior of man in respect to it, or, will nature end up fooling us? At the same time: "mente lamenta?" This other play of words unites the words "la menta," meaning mint, to form the word "lamenta," meaning lament, after the word "mente," which may mean either to lie, or the mind. The question becomes, does the human mind lament this situation of devastation or is it unconscious of the dangers we are facing?

The uncertainty facing the future of the world and humanity is demonstrated in the installation through four elements that alternate feelings of pessimism and optimism. A void, represented by a round hollow full of water, is the "black tide," the mystery of the future, the new millennium. In fact, the water is not transparent, but cloudy, dark, covered by a dense layer of charcoal pieces floating on the surface. A wooden catwalk, also round, runs along the entire outside perimeter of the pond and symbolizes the raft man depends on when facing the uncertain. A setting composed of structures that seem like big cushions wrap around the catwalk and the pond. Made with mesh and iron wool, these elements represent the complexity of the modern world and the materialization of its various shades. But from this darkness emerges a sign of optimism: from water itself, nature is born, symbolized by small aquatic mint plants that, with their delicate smell and their bright green color, send an unequivocal message of reconquest over contamination on the part of nature itself, good over evil.

This temporary garden is composed around a pool of water surrounded by a wooden catwalk. Metallic three-dimensional shapes are delicately supported by mint plants

Photomontage

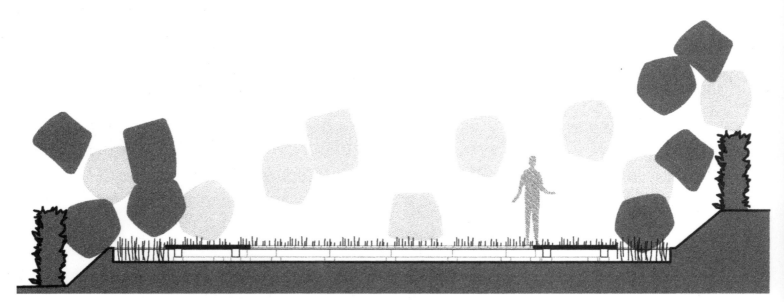

Section

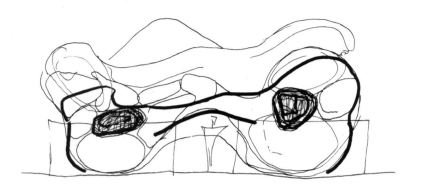

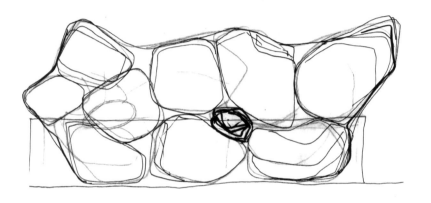

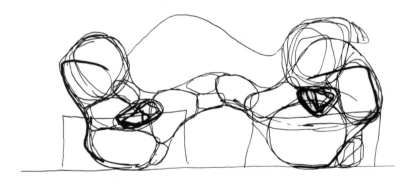

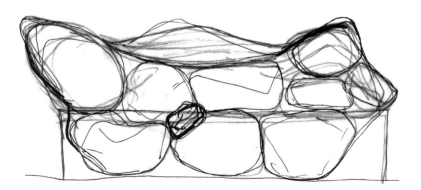

Sketches

Nature is represented by aquatic mint plants. These rise right through the
center of the pool and form a "bel" around it to counteract against the
water's black color and the gray color of the metallic mesh structures.

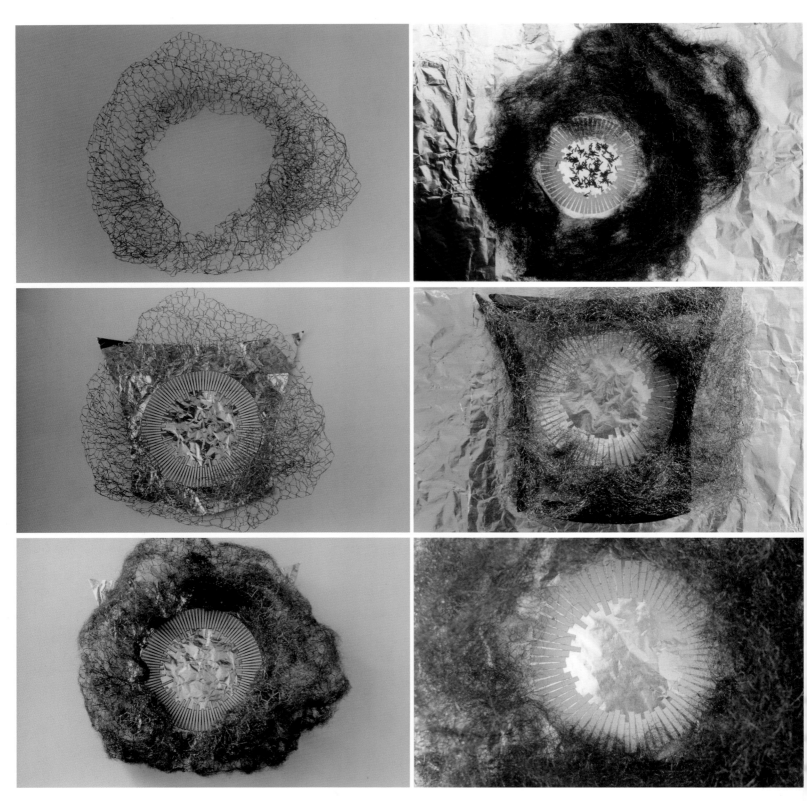

Models

Photo © Annie Ypperciel, Claude Cormier Architectes Paysagistes

Solange

Lyons, France   2003

LANDSCAPE ARCHITECTS
Claude Cormier Architectes Paysagistes

CLIENT
Domaine Lacroix-Laval

AREA
1 acre

Claude Cormier was born on a small farm in the area east of the state of Quebec. Since childhood, his relationship with natural surroundings was determined by the necessities of life in the country, so much so that he became bored with it. Only after his studies in Agronomy did he realize that what interested him was not plant genetics but finding a way to transform nature into something more attractive and even fun. This is how Cormier decides to dedicate himself to the architecture of the landscape. He started with an investigation and a very personal path, where focus on the historical, ecological, geological and even sociological are united with a firm intention to transform the world of vegetation into a more pleasurable expression than is typical of its reality. Artifice is a fundamental point of his work: it's not about making a setting in its most natural state possible; it's about doing the opposite, taking natural materials and expressing them in an artificial and surprising way. The strong ecological will of the landscaper is combined with a focus on stage-design that revolutionizes the norm and forces the spectator to reconsider their certainties and their outlook towards nature itself. The playful creations use the natural and the artificial to suggest a different perspective, oftentimes fun, of the countryside.

The installation created in Domaine Lacroix-Laval, near Lyons, for the fourth edition of the International Festival of Gardens of Métis, clearly follows the same thought. Inside a hundred-year-old forest, Cormier creates a type of vertical garden by upholstering the tree trunks with artificial flowers. There are fifteen trunks over 20 feet high, with sixteen thousand pink, white and red artificial flowers. It's not about planting or utilizing natural flora, it's about surprising with silk fabrications that, on the one hand, reflect the constructed nature of the countryside and, on the other, inspire themselves in the important textiles tradition of the city of Lyons.

Photomontage

Photo © Simon Wood

Amoeba 2

Martin Place, Sydney, Australia   2004

LANDSCAPE ARCHITECTS
McGregor & Partners

CLIENT
Australian Institute of Landscape Architects

PARTNERS
Royal Botanical Gardens, Sydney & AILA NSW

AREA
adaptive

COST
6,800 euros

On the 28th of December, 2004, Martin Place, a pedestrian avenue in Sydney, awoke to find itself overrun by one hundred thirty-two peculiar amoeba cells. It was nothing more or less than a bunch of painted tires, the center of which, or the nucleus, had been arranged with Stratum Green, a material elaborated completely from recycled tires to serve as soil replacement for lawns. On these amoeba cell lawns, the city's gardeners placed obsolete sprinklers as a statement in favor of a reduction in water consumption. With this installation, McGregor & Partners were calling the spectators' attention to the more than one hundred thousand tires destined for the garbage every year in the state of New South Wales. Ultimately, the goal was to demonstrate that sustainable growth in the cities is achieved through the use of available resources, particularly waste materials, and not in the expansion of an unchecked environmental footprint. For the architects, existing infrastructures, including those that are abandoned or in disuse, offer sufficient possibilities for use and regeneration, reason to resist the creation of newer ones and their consequent cost or the absorption of resources from adjacent areas. Created for Environment Day, which was announced by the Royal Botanical Gardens, this particular army of tires created an efficient form of urban impact.

The Amoeba 2 project also consisted of an initial phase that launched a series of mobile gardens towed by hybrid eco-vehicles, constructed of recycled steel, wooden beams and water. Intrinsically loyal to the spirit of use and re-use that inspired it; once the installation was dismantled the Amoeba 2 cells reappeared at the botanical gardens as part of the Gardens of the Future show. This time the tires were grouped together into two horrendous piles that attempted to spark the audience's conscience regarding the large volume of garbage our societies generate and the contamination that results from their final destiny at the garbage dump.

Amoeba 2, an efficient and powerful way of alerting spectators to the amount of waste generated in cities and the important place recycling has in guaranteeing sustainable urban growth. The individual cells, pneumatic and gardened, overran the most emblematic streets in the center of Sydney in honor of Environment Day.

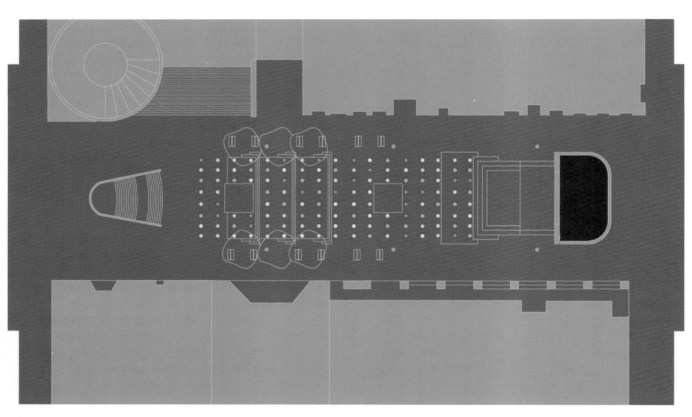

Plan

Rendering

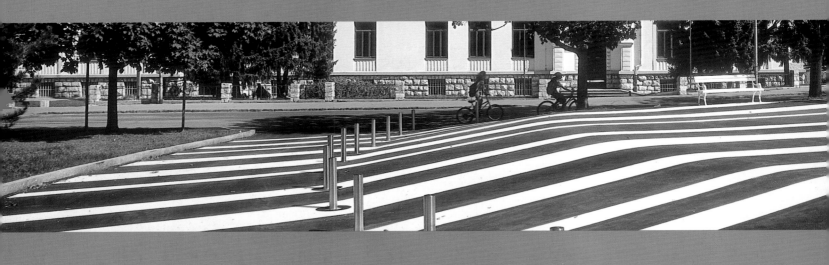

Squares

01   Das Águas Square
Campinas, Brazil

02   Royal Victoria Square
London, United Kingdom

03   Festplassen
Bergen, Norway

04   Renovation of Čufarjev Square
Jesenice, Slovenija

05   Aristide Briand Square
Valence, France

06   François Mitterrand Square
Creusot, France

07   Kreuzlingen Hafenplatz
Kreuzlingen, Switzerland

08   Incontro Tra i Popoli Square
Settimo Milanese, Italy

09   Vittorio Veneto Square
Galliate, Italy

10   Square Four Garden
Beirut, Lebanon

11   Saitama Plaza
Saitama, Japan

12   Manukau Square
Manukau, New Zealand

Photo © Dal Pian Arquitetos

Das Águas Square

Campinas, Brazil   2004

LANDSCAPE ARCHITECTS
Dal Pian Arquitetos

CLIENT
Sociedade de Abastecimento de Água e Saneamento de Campinas SANASA

PARTNERS
Renato Dal Pian, Lilian Dal Pian (authors); Pablo Chakur, Carolina Pons, Fernanda Ferreira, Filomena Piscoletta (others)

AREA
57,049 SF

This plaza is the result of a contest held by a drinking water company in the Brazilian city of Campinas. This is the rehabilitation of a water tank located near a central area. The contest called for the transformation of this architectural structure—built in 1889 and unused at this time—within a cultural center that holds open spaces. The project was resolved with a sequence of openly constructed areas that integrate not only with themselves but with the urban fabric surrounding them. In particular, the plaza is configured as a completely clear expanse on the three sides that complete the block of space that constitutes the intervention. The inspiration for its design comes from water itself. Its presence is central, though not expressed in monumental fashion: quite the opposite, it's manifested through more or less programmed and predicted events.

The plaza is proposed as a walkable space in any direction and its design is marked by a set of parallel axes that contain the few elements presented: water, vegetation and seating. These three functional lines interrupt the ground's continuous surface, paved with slabs of gray stone. The lines of water are expressed in two different ways. In one, a mirror of still waters has been built to serve as a line marking the edge of the constructed area and offers a space for peace and contemplation. In the other, a series of fountains sprout directly from the ground in the center of the plaza, creating a transparent barrier of motion. The stone benches are arranged one behind the other under the vegetation's partial shade, which acts as a filter between the plaza and the city.

The rehabilitation of the block, proposed by one of the city's drinking water companies, has given shape to an open public space where the presence of water is central without becoming grandiose. The plaza is built around parallel lines, each representing a basic element of the project: water, in two different presentations–still and moving–and shade provided by the vegetation.

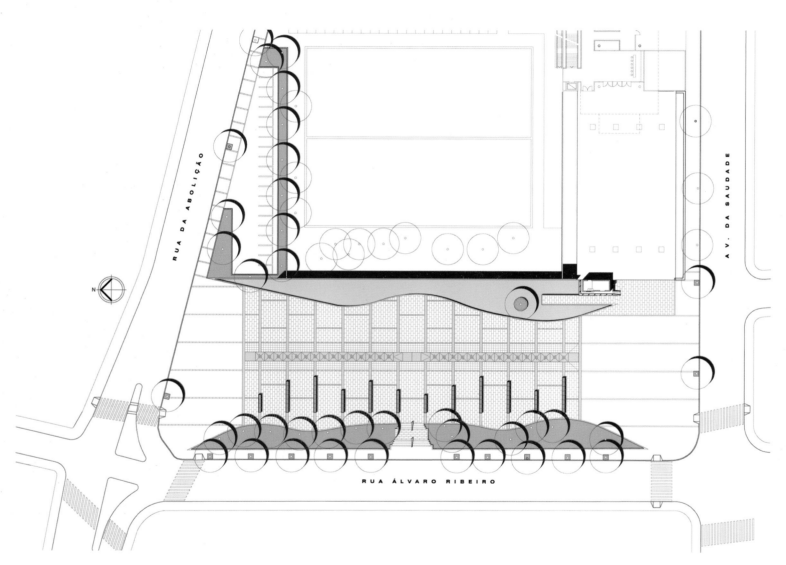

Plan

Section

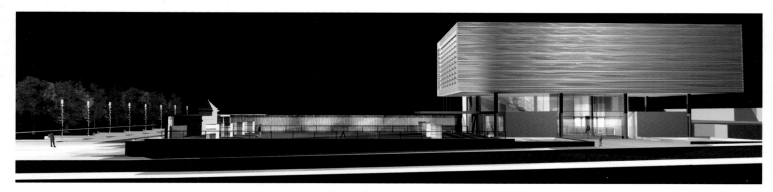

Elevation

Photo © Dixi Carrillo/EDWA; Peter Matthews

Royal Victoria Square

London, United Kingdom   2000

LANDSCAPE ARCHITECTS
EDAW

CLIENT
London Development Agency

PARTNERS
Patel Taylor Architects (arquitects); Aspen Burrow Crocker (structural engineering); Aspen Burrow Crocker (mechanical and electrical engineer); Tweeds (quantity surveyor); Fitzpatrick Contractors Ltd (contractor)

AREA
2.5 acres

COST
4,665,000 euros

The royal walls situated on the shores of the Thames River suffered a period of abandon and neglect when the terminals for maritime traffic were moved out of London in the 1970s. Left behind like ghostly witnesses of a bygone era, the vast cement extensions upon which stood factories and warehouses, the old cranes and the thin road that covered the area were denied their function. In recent years, the London Development Agency has embarked on an ambitious project to recuperate this area running alongside the river. Towards that goal, and coinciding with the construction of a new pedestrian bridge over the dock, they hired Patel Taylor and the EDAW studio to design the square. The idea was to provide a public space with quality and innovation to an urban area that is fast rising to be an important residential, economic and entertainment center. The plan clears access to the river and incorporates the head of the bridge as well as the esplanade adjacent to the East London Exhibition Centre (ExCeL), for which it provides an open-air exposition space. This way, the narrow ports are replaced by a huge central square with a slightly inclined grass esplanade, flanked by two long steel projections.

The path to the ExCeL building is lined with quiet fountains that confer solemnity to the entrance and serve as interactive diversion for children on hot days. The setting's historical identity is highlighted with a wise archaeological-industrial treatment: various cranes and warehouses have survived the renovation and the metallic structures are inscribed with the names of some of the boats that once moored here; the masts of which also evoke a unique field of dynamic poles. The construction materials selected obey the same historical purpose—steel, natural stone, cement and wood—joined to the old docks but used in an innovative fashion. The Royal Victoria Square's success lies not only in the careful details, but in its ability to preserve a human scale in such a vast space.

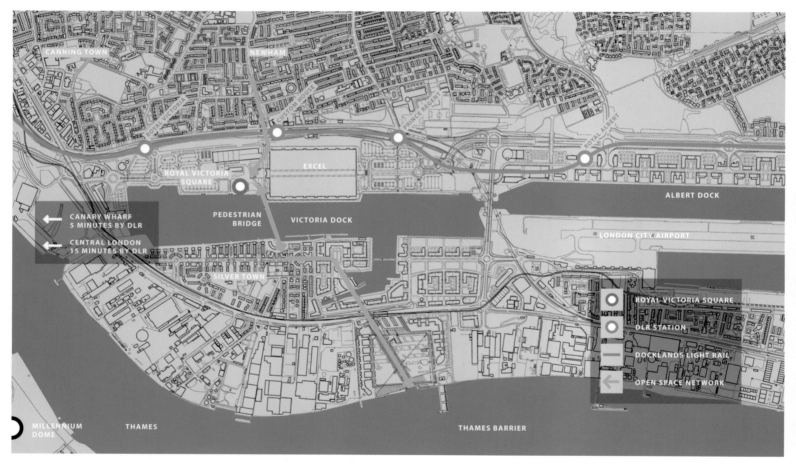

CANNING TOWN

NEWHAM

CUSTOM HOUSE

PRINCE REGENT

ROYAL VICTORIA

ROYAL ALBERT

EXCEL

ROYAL VICTORIA SQUARE

ALBERT DOCK

CANARY WHARF
5 MINUTES BY DLR

CENTRAL LONDON
15 MINUTES BY DLR

PEDESTRIAN BRIDGE

VICTORIA DOCK

LONDON CITY AIRPORT

SILVER TOWN

ROYAL VICTORIA SQUARE

DLR STATION

DOCKLANDS LIGHT RAIL

OPEN SPACE NETWORK

MILLENNIUM DOME

THAMES

THAMES BARRIER

Site Plan

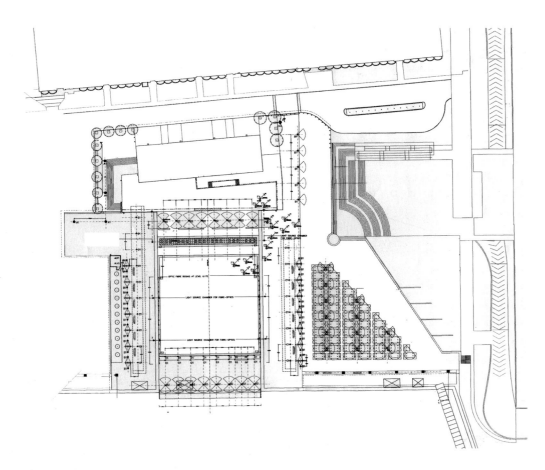

Plan

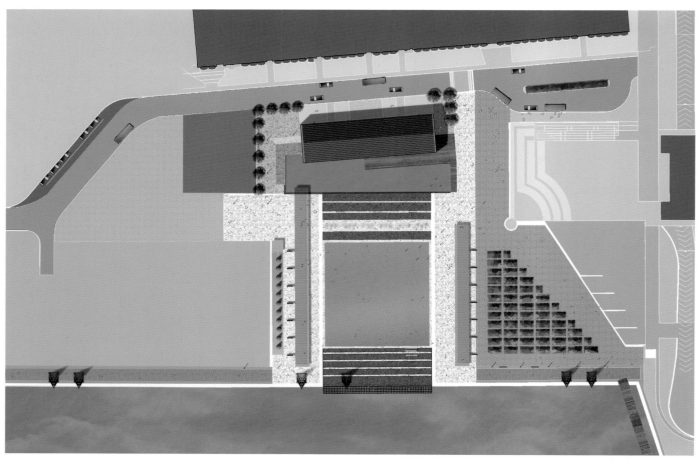

Rendered Plan

Photo © Arne Sælen

Festplassen

Bergen, Norway   2003

LANDSCAPE ARCHITECTS
Landskap Design

CLIENT
City of Bergen

PARTNERS
Arne Sælen (chief designer and planning supervisor)

AREA
55,972 SF

COST
3,500,000 euros

Surrounded by seven hills, the Norwegian city of Bergen occupies a privileged natural enclave and is the doorway to the Norwegian Fjords. On its main axis, beside a pretty lake and facing south, opens the Festplassen (festival plaza). For the planning stage, the architects at the Landskap Design studio were inspired by the discernable majesty of the countryside. On its perimeter they've reproduced the silhouette of the towering elevations that have sheltered the city. For this, bordering the lake and covering a total surface of an acre and a half, they've employed various polished granite walls in step-ladder fashion to evoke the inclination and separation of the surrounding mountains, a mimicry highlighted by a bordering crown of stainless steel.

The plaza's orientation and the materials chosen interact in a studied and delicate manner. Facing south, the plaza looks out on the reflections created by the sun against the water and these are extended over the streaks in the gray granite esplanade. Some

of the slabs, in fact, have been treated to achieve an appearance similar to black marble. Because of the plaza's slight incline, it was necessary to install drains of solid stone that were sunken by one inch. Once filtered, the water is cleared through four bronze drain pipes within each drain.

Access on each side of the plaza consists of four giant stairways that connect by way of walkways flanked by cherry trees and are adjacent to the parks. The stairs possess different textures and their surfaces have been given alternate treatments. Also, the twelve inch steps have a special relief with the aim of facilitating movement for people with little or no sight.

Lastly, eight slender lampposts illuminate the space with controlled LED light systems, effectively reducing energy consumption to ten times less than that of the common spotlight. The polycarbonate circuit cables are placed between the granite steps so that at night they seem suspended in air.

The Bergen Festplassen opens a well-lit space on a typical Norwegian waterfront with wooden houses painted lively colors and descends along a soft incline towards the gray waters of the lake. The cement walls with a stainless steel finish help to integrate the piece with its surroundings by evoking the crests atop the seven surrounding mountains that are visible from the plaza.

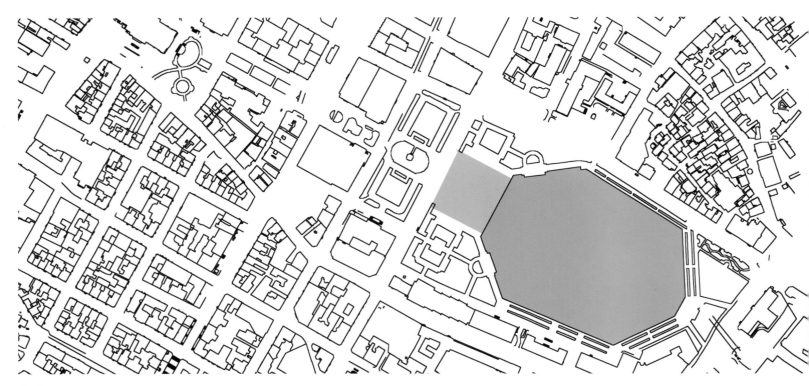

Site Plan

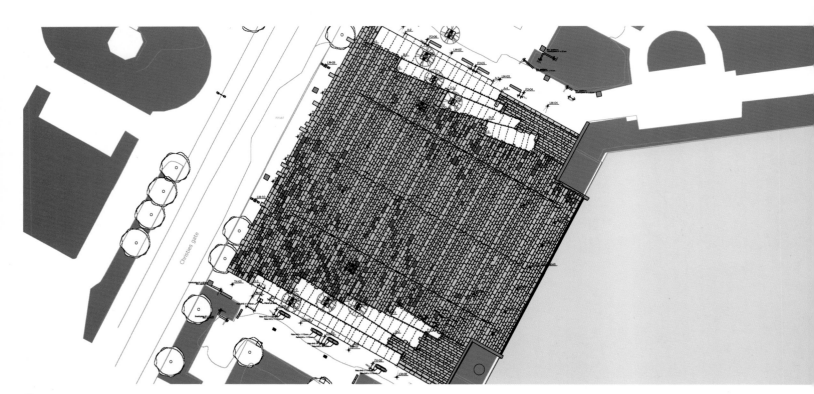

Plan

Photo © Miran Kambič

Renovation of Čufarjev Square

Jesenice, Slovenija   2003

LANDSCAPE ARCHITECTS
Scapelab

CLIENT
Municipality of Jesenice

PARTNERS
Marko Studen (architect); Metek Kučina (landscape architect)

AREA
43,056 SF

COST
250,000 euros

The remodeling of Čufarjev Square in the Slovenian city of Jesenice began with the conviction that over time, even the smallest elements could be used as agents for transforming its surroundings. With a small surface area, the project at hand embraces many large-scale architectural categories such as urban design, landscape architecture, ecology and economy.

What the town hall leaders had in mind when they organized their contest was to build a traditional square with a fountain. The chosen project didn't exactly meet their initial idea, even though the plaza is conceived as an open public space and has very evident water presence.

Surrounded by two roads and public buildings such as a library, a theater, a school and a cinema, this 43,056-square-foot triangular plaza occupies a central area in the life of the city. This public disposition relies on the constant presence of diverse social groups who all make the place particularly lively. The

project aims to emphasize this aspect even more: it creates a space capable of holding events as varied as an open-air market, music concerts and art installations. It's an empty plaza where people and their movements are the leading protagonists, while street fixtures are located in peripheral positions.

In the central part, this multi-functional space becomes integrated with water, a presence that is both visible and invisible, coming straight out of the ground without any intermediate structures or computer-controlled pumps and valves. The choice of materials is rather modest, making the intervention closer to a work of road maintenance than an urban remodeling plan: the plaza has been paved with black asphalt and then painted white. The surface looks like a board with a giant pedestrian crossway than can be refreshed in the future by simply changing its color.

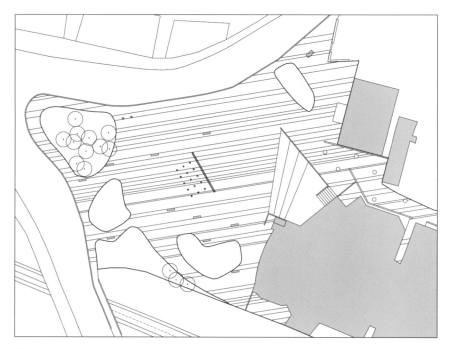

Plan

Photomontage

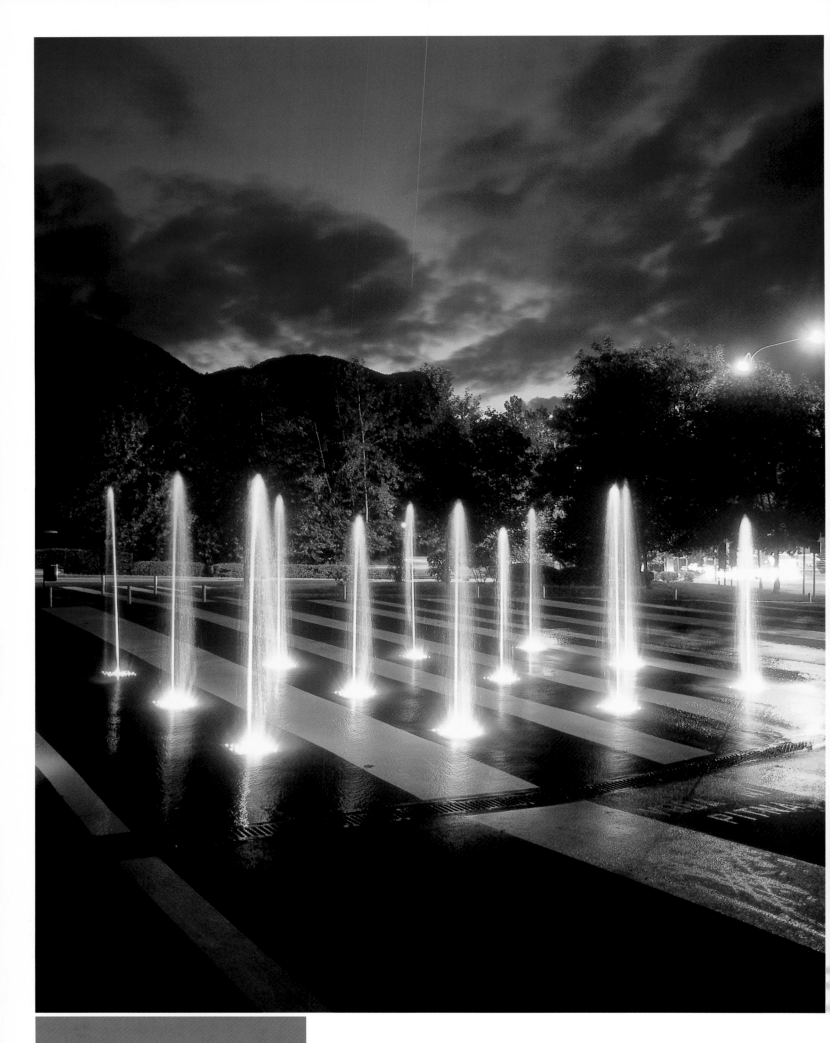

Photo © Agence APS, Deval Photo

Aristide Briand Square

Valence, France   2004

LANDSCAPE ARCHITECTS
Agence APS Paysagistes DPLG Associés

CLIENT
Ville de Valence

PARTNERS
Atelier Lumière, CAP VERT Ingénierie, BET Paysage (design team); Enterprise 26, Jardins de Provence, ETDE, Enterprise Gascheau, Enterprise Appia, Mochal Granits, Sportiello, Enterprise Oboussier, Maia Sonnier/ATF (general contractor)

AREA
72,118 SF

COST
2,000,000 euros

Aristide Briand Square is located in Valence, a small university city in the southeast part of France, and forms part of a series of projects undertaken by the landscapers at a local studio called Agence APS to rehabilitate the urban center. The specificity of the space's context and morphology, like the limitations set by the authorities, required an appropriate solution that would combine originality with elegance. The project was primarily based on reinforcing the importance of an avenue that starts at the station, unites with the Champ de Mars rotunda, a park beside the square, and empties out at the gardens that flank the Rodano River. This way the avenue regains its relevance as a historic engine of this part of the city's development and the plaza, urban center and the riverside are all connected. The plaza entrance on the Champ de Mars side is open to the setting sun and connects to 7.5 acres of open public spaces with vegetation, while the buildings that surround its western and northern sides protect it from the cold northwest winds. The space that arises between the reconvert-

ed avenue and the Champ de Mars esplanade is used for two different objectives. A parking lot alleviates congestion and the typical urban problem of limited parking. At the same time, a palm grove set atop a wood surface makes for a pleasant meeting point and evokes Valence's Mediterranean spirit. The twenty-six palm trees from China create shade for the groups of two and three benches placed on the wooden surface. A small canal that passes through the center of the square recalls the cultural inheritance of Valence and the Rodano River. The water makes a refreshing sound as it displaces the pebbles on its bottom, extracted from the riverbed itself, and as it streams out of the eight fountains protruding from the elliptical pond. This place's historic and symbolic perception becomes poetic with nightfall, when the starry sky and the artificial lighting reciprocate to prolong the imaginary trip through the space.

Photomontage (aereal view)

Once connected, the square and the Champ de Mars gardens form a
public esplanade of over 322,917 square feet to facilitate the transition
from urban center to river landscape. In the center of the square a small
canal was placed to evoke the city's cultural heritage.

Elevations

Photo © François Tribel, Services Techniques Ville du Creusot, Jean Max Llorca

François Mitterrand Square

Creusot, France   2005

LANDSCAPE ARCHITECTS
*François Tribel/Atelier Grunig Tribel, JML
Arquitectura del Agua*

CLIENT
Ville du Creusot

PARTNERS
*Jean Max Llorca (principal in charge); Nicolas
Llense, Stéphane Llorca (others); Guy Marie
Lambert, P. Massé (engineering)*

AREA
17,222 SF

"Coeur de ville" (heart of the city) is the name given this project, which was launched in the French city of Creusot in 2004 to recuperate the urban center. The area of intervention covers a surface area of 17,222 square feet and extends from the town hall to the great esplanade of François Mitterrand Square. From the start of the design process an objective was decided to give water itself a central function so that its qualities could be exalted and its presence would be constant throughout. With this goal, the space was reorganized as an integral part of the urban ensemble in which it is located. Another requirement was that the water be seen or heard at all times from any point on the esplanade.

Come time to delineate and diversify the different functions of the spaces and their distribution, treatment of the surfaces became the solution. That way, the different types of granite were laid out in a way that would

mark the function of each area of the square, distinguishing pedestrian areas from those destined for the circulation of vehicular traffic. With this, integration with vehicular traffic was achieved in a harmonious and discrete fashion. On the other hand, this granite carpet, with its subtly differentiated gray colors, becomes compact and monolithic and serves as a visual nexus for articulating and integrating the diverse architectural structures that circle the square. Aside from the pavement, the water fountains constitute another element in the project's design that contributes to the configuration of the spaces and the functions of the square. Visible or audible across the entire square, they create calm perspectives, promote interaction among passersby— especially the smaller ones—and, in the hotter months of the year, promote a sense of agreeable and continual freshness.

Water is a constant in François Mitterrand Square. Visible and audible from any part, it invites passersby, especially children, to interact with the public space. The pavement over which the water continuously flows is carefully treated with granite that generates different textures to delineate the use of each space.

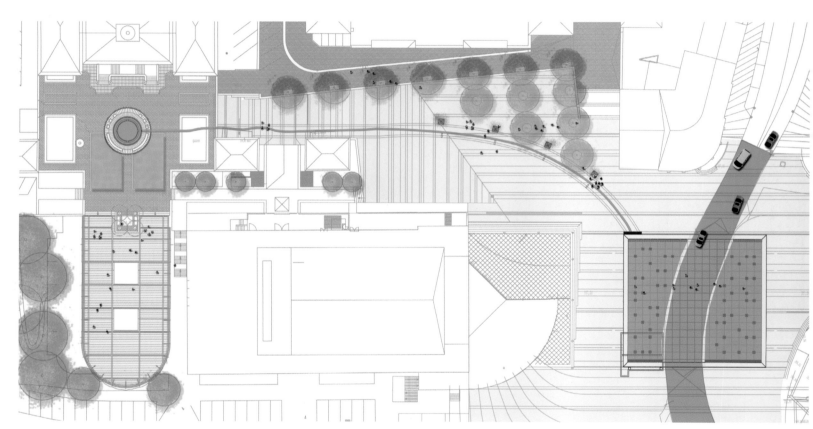

Plan

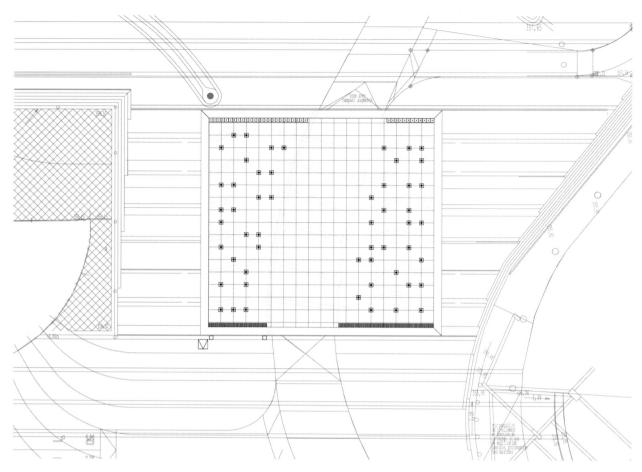

Square Plan

Photo © Giosanna Crivelli, Paolo L. Bürgi, D. Florentine Schmidt

Kreuzlingen Hafenplatz

Kreuzlingen, Switzerland   2003

LANDSCAPE ARCHITECTS
Paolo L. Bürgi

CLIENT
City of Kreuzlingen

PARTNERS
Planimpuls AG Civil Engineers (consultant)

AREA
191,598 SF

COST
880,700 euros

The city of Kreuzlingen, in the northeast of Switzerland, has always been narrowly linked to the lake of the same name beside it. With the start of the new century, a project was put into effect to redefine this relationship; until this moment, the development of the lake had always been somewhat spontaneous, lacking unity or systematic planning. The proposal by Paolo L. Bürgi permits the creation of a new connection between city and lake and vice versa, especially for those who cross the lake to get to the city. Laid out as a square beside the lake, the plaza is a reference point that permits the contemplation of the expanse of water, its surroundings and the horizon. This way, two axes connect land with water, urban space with nature.

The square consists of an open cement esplanade with stairways that descend a smooth incline all the way into and below the water's surface. Cement benches, painted in attractive but not strident colors, invite passersby to sit and rest for a while and enjoy the landscape, from early in the morning when the fishing boats go out, until much later when the numerous recreational boats cross the waters. Motifs have been recorded into the pavement of the square, making reference to the life, history, culture and occupations of Kreuzlingen, not to mention its traditional commitment to the environment. A fountain, also of cement, recalls a canal that has slowly eroded the surface over which it passes. For night lighting, various physical and optical criteria were applied; on the plaza floor, various points of light reflect the starry sky.

The square, which has various colorful benches seving as scenic viewpoints, not only redefines the relation of the city with its lakefront, but also offers a new gateway to those traveling over the lake. The stepped-seating recalls that which the sea produces on the sand of the beach.

0   10   50m

Plan

A concrete fountain, a constant in the work of Paolo L. Bürgi, decorates the plaza in Kreuzlingen. The flowing water represents a canal that has eroded its riverbed to form a small canyon. The architect has recorded motifs in the pavement that evoke the daily life and history of the country.

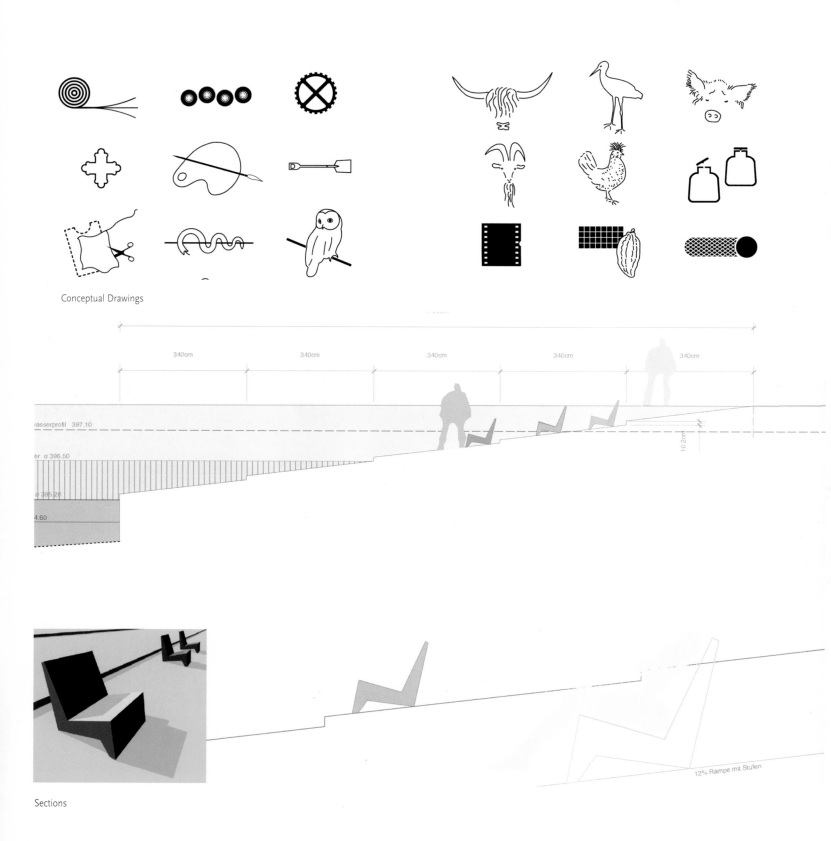

Conceptual Drawings

Sections

Photo © De Amicis Architetti

Incontro Tra i Popoli Square

Settimo Milanese, Italy   2003

LANDSCAPE ARCHITECTS
De Amicis Architetti

CLIENT
Comune di Settimo Milanese

PARTNERS
Federico Mazza, Micaela Montorfano, Paolo Moretto, Eugenia Silvestri

AREA
75,347 SF

Settimo Milanese is a city center located on the periphery of Milan and, like many other conurbations of large cities, must conscientiously fight to preserve the independence of its urban and cultural idiosyncrasies. Because of this, a part of the spirit that launched the contest held by local government in 1997 was an attempt to prevent the Lombard capital from becoming a commuter place. De Amicis studio took charge of the project with a landscape plan that recovered the idea of using public space as a central axis with purpose for the entire city. The project was not without difficulties, considering that the construction of the square was owed to a contractual obligation the promoter had to fulfill in order to be awarded the go ahead to build an underground parking lot.

The context in which the transformation had to operate was typical of these circumstances: a succession of linear blocks of homes and enclosed grounds where the only public spaces were destined to traffic, thus creating a lack of reference points. Incontro Tra i Popoli Square (meeting between towns square) resolves these problems with a centripetal design that permits the construction of new spatial identity and creates a new set of relations with its surroundings. For this, various architectural resources were used, like shelters, illuminated walls and fixed furniture (tables, chairs, etcetera), circular benches that surround the tree pits and green hedges. This achieves a functional distribution of space that distinguishes between small plots of land, delineated by low walls that facilitate and promote get-togethers, and an area of circulation with the histotical city hall building in the distance. The assignment's limitations, a respect for the concept that drove it and the surroundings motivated the humble materials chosen for the project; unpolished finishes like copper, corten steel, Lessinia stone, pine and Indian porphyry.

The simplicity and sobriety of the materials used doesn't prohibit even a
bit of modernity and originality. The illuminated and projected walls
create and delineate areas for meeting areas and other diverse activities.

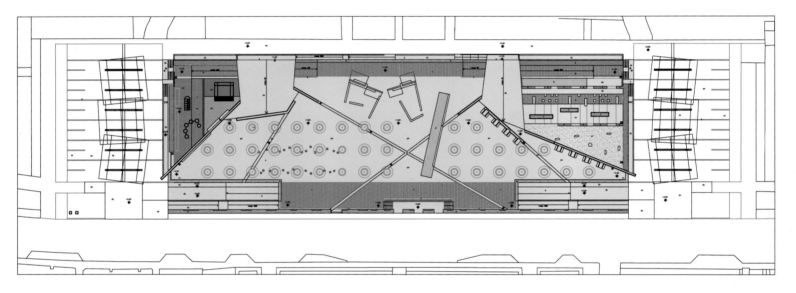

Plan

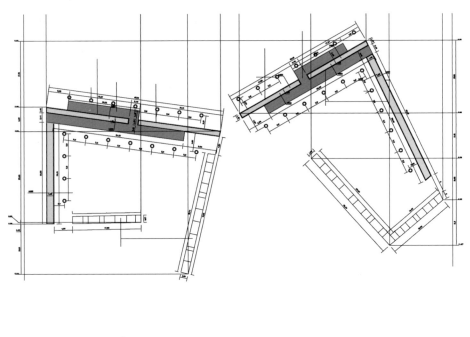

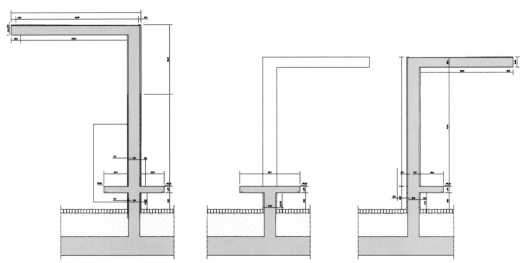

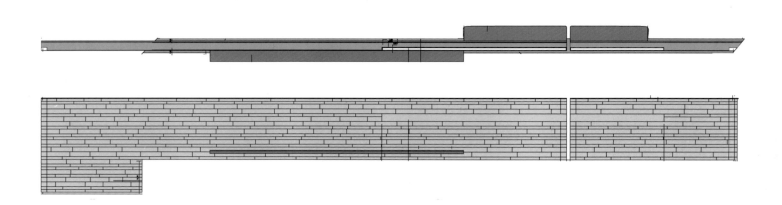

Construction Details

Photo © Pietro Carrieri

Vittorio Veneto Square

Galliate, Italy   2004

LANDSCAPE ARCHITECTS
Studio Lazzaretto

CLIENT
Amministrazione Comunale di Galliate (Novara)

PARTNER
Antonio Lazzaretto (principal in charge); Maurizio Garrazi (assistant); Luisa Bellini, Annamaria Cristofoli (consultants); Mariano Barbuscia (structure); Stefano Romanoni (security)

AREA
137,778 SF

COST
1,498,000 euros

Vittorio Veneto Square, in the Italian locality of Galliate, comprises a succession of adjacent esplanades within the urban limits and a noble Sforza castle. This type of open space is today still identified with the term "terraggio" and its configuration corresponds to the ancient urban regulations of the Roman Empire. From the start of this project, the architects assumed a need to preserve this inherited characteristic and they planned a sober and unified rehabilitation, one that would suggest minimum intervention with aims to make no attack on the place's singular identity.

From this conception, the irregularity of the perimeter was respected and, with the same intention, they managed to give the expansion joints an uneven design, in such a way that they reproduced the naturally brittle cement in analogy with the mix of gravel and compacted earth that used to cover the place. Before being poured, the pavement was joined in place with aggregate from the Tesino riverbed.

The most palpable part of the intervention corresponds to the building with two vaulted structures that marks the entrance to an underground parking lot and a glass-fronted bar that allows a clear view of the castle. A fine veil of water descends continuously over the mosaic that covers one of the entrance walls. The dressings on this structure, even the copper, offer a light counterpoint to the context. The rest of the elements are integrated with subtle discretion, from the white granite path that permits passage around the perimeter of the plaza in front of the castle moat, to the vegetation.

Various acacias refresh and protect the plaza entrance on the Scurolo side and a proud Paulonia symbolically marks the border with the adjacent Plaza of the Martyrs. Finally, for the lighting it was decided to keep the traditional lampposts already in place and an irregular mesh of lights was added at ground level to serve a double function: create a suggestive atmosphere at night and show the position of the weekly market during daylight hours.

The most important part of the intervention is the two structures that allow access to the parking lot and the bar. The linear and compact vaulted structures contrast with the picturesque urban surroundings; the glass wall of the bar offers splendid views of the castle and the church.

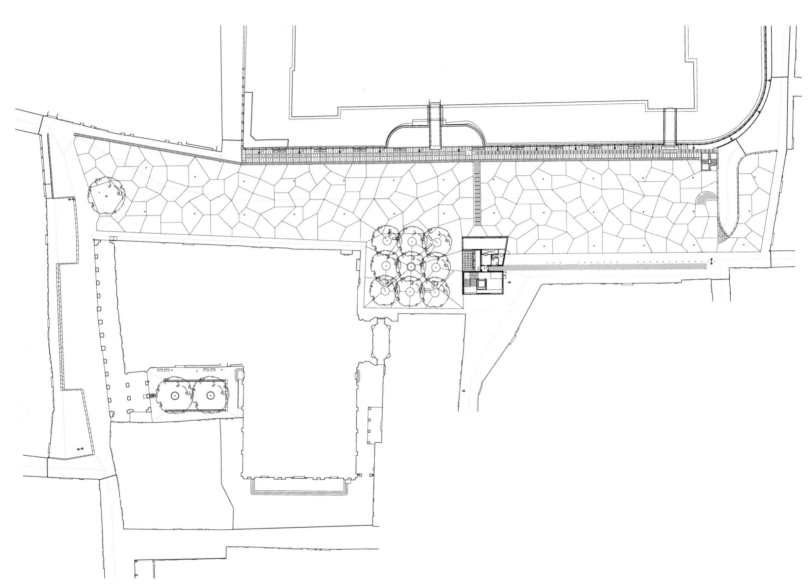

Plan

From the start of the project, the architects stated a will that the intervention reflect the traditionally historic construction given this locale. A priority focus in the rehabilitation of the plaza was unity itself. To achieve it, two basic materials were used, porphyry stone and granite.

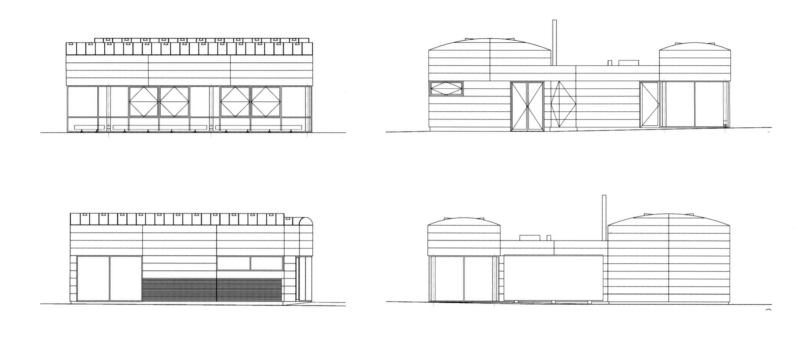

Sections

Photo © Matteo Piazza

Square Four Garden

Beirut, Lebanon   2004

LANDSCAPE ARCHITECTS
Vladimir Djurovic Landscape Architecture

CLIENT
*Société Libanaise de Développement et
Reconstruction (Solidere)*

PARTNERS
*AG Contracting (contractor and engineer); Light
Box (lighting); Hydrelec (water specialist)*

AREA
8,773 SF

Located right in the center of Beirut, at the start of emblematic Weygand Street, the Square Four public garden is a peaceful pool of beauty and history. It serves as a warm welcome to foreigners and locals who enter the heart of this renovated city, an important Mediterranean port and an intellectual luminary of the Arabic world of yesteryear. The delicate composition of the space revolves around two very old ficus trees that contain a powerful symbolic meaning: both trees, native to the area and veterans of a thousand battles and ups and downs, are witnesses to the rich history of this city and its people. Their silhouettes seem to sprout from the wooden floorboards that have been placed on a small hill of grass; the boards have been carefully cut and fitted around the irregular outline of the trees. Entry is granted by way of a lateral stairway.

Serving as frame around the ficus trees, a rectangular square with a huge bench of sculptured stone measuring 66 feet long invites relaxation. In front of it, a mirror of water is raised to reflect the silhouettes of the adjacent buildings, the An-Nahar building among them. It's an intelligent and beautiful means of contextualizing the park and making it participate with its surroundings while serving as a place of escape and refuge. The garden, in genuine Arabic tradition, is a delight for the senses. It pays homage to the city and its history, but also to nature and the therapeutic power of beauty. The constant and serene murmur of water falling over serrated stone and the varied hues that develop at dusk, nuances of light and shade, are proof of this. At nightfall, time seems to condense to the point of stopping, accentuating the weighted meaning of these two trees that, like inscrutable warriors or guardians, remind those who contemplate them of Beirut's aged roots and its nontransferable identity.

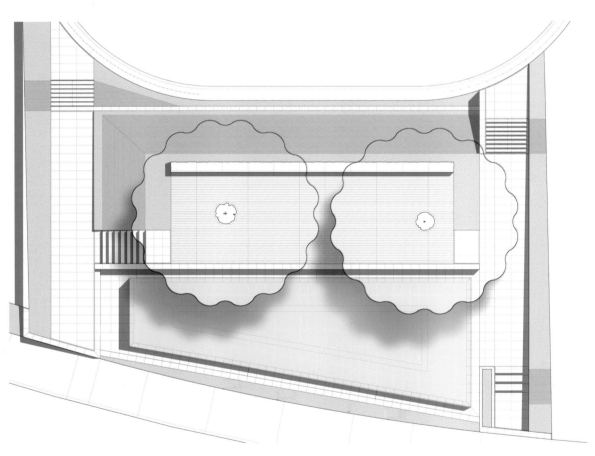

Plan

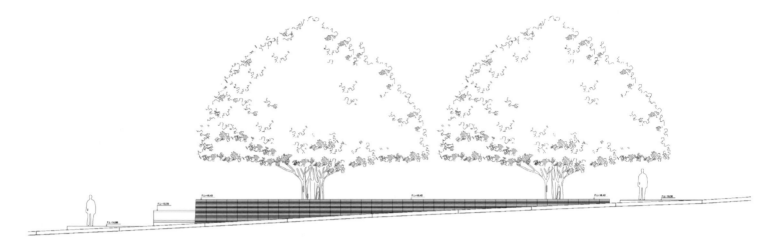

Elevation

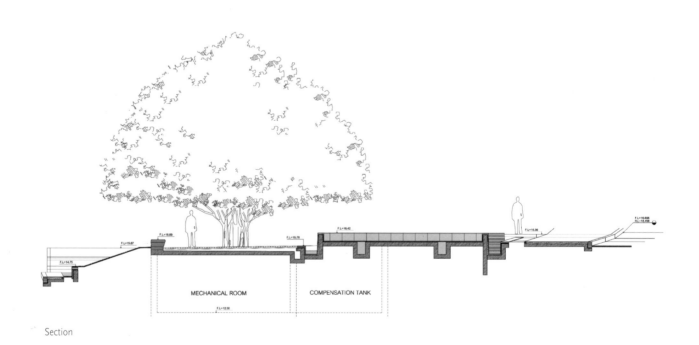

MECHANICAL ROOM   COMPENSATION TANK

Section

Photo © PWP Landscape Architecture

Saitama Plaza

Saitama, Japan   2000

LANDSCAPE ARCHITECTS
PWP Landscape Architecture

CLIENT
Saitama Prefectural Government

PARTNERS
Ohtori Consultants, NTT Urban Development Co (consultants)

AREA
5 acres

The plaza rises out of the pedestrian core of a new area of Tokyo called Saitama. This area, object of a 1994 contest, houses a Super Arena, the city's largest train station, a skyscraper and hundreds of acres of offices, homes and commercial space. The plaza is located on the roof of a 30-foot-high glass office building.

The project is inspired by a forest sacred to Shintoists. For the newly conceived plaza, a portion of this forest on the outskirts of Tokyo has been reproduced. The idea is to cut out a corner of tranquility and serenity and transport it to the chaotic center of the city. The space is almost square, with a surface formed by a dense grid that becomes a paving of cast-aluminum grills alternated with strips of gray stone. On this surface, two hundred twenty zelkova trees, Japan's most popular species, create a continuous awning thanks to their particular shape. These trees are planted in supports rooted in five feet of special soil. The suspended

paving system was carefully designed to drain rainwater, which is filtered through the aluminum grates to the lowest level of the floor, where it is accumulated and drained. At street level are four glass towers that rise from the commercial building and break the homogenous awning created by the trees. These structures contain stairs, elevators, a café and a restaurant. There is also a small police booth, a green area for the children to play in and a glass-floored area for music and dance that is transformed into an ice-skating rink in the winter. Between the rows of zelkova trees, a system of wooden benches surrounds set-in panels for cultural announcements. Lighting comes from these panels, from the glass-floored area, from the towers and from beneath the grills in the floor. Stairs are located on each open side of the elevated plaza, while the connections with the neighboring buildings and the train station facilitate the movement of large masses of people.

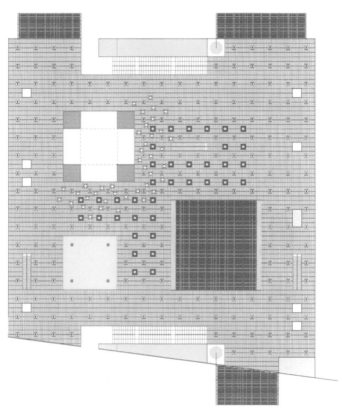

Plan

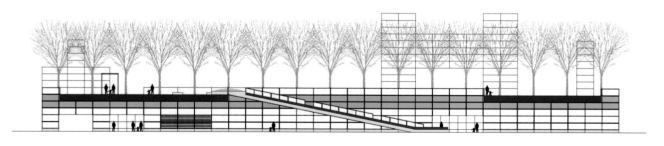

Section

Photo © Simon Devitt

Manukau Square

Manukau, New Zealand   2005

LANDSCAPE ARCHITECTS
David Irwin/Isthmus Group

CLIENT
Manukau City Council

PARTNERS
*Tim Fitzpatrick, Orson Waldock, Lee Brazier,
Diane Brand (urban design); Rewi Thompson
(concept architecture); GHD (civil engineering);
E-Cubed (structural engineering); Dempsey &
Wood Civil Contractor (contractor)*

AREA
77,500 SF

COST
1,629,600 euros

Manukau is the third most populated city in New Zealand. Its urban center was constructed in the 1970s in accord with an urban development plan that was added to in the 1980s. Nevertheless, fifteen years later, this space did not adequately reflect the vitality and dynamism of the city and its inhabitants, having clearly become outdated. When it came time to face the renovation of the civic center to transform it into an extroverted space, the members of the Isthmus Group decided to begin with plurality, the multicultural composition characteristic of Manukau and its inhabitants. This premise was developed and communicated through the design's abstraction, the variety of the materials used and an extreme care for details. The result is an intrinsically civic space with many possibilities for informal use, both contemporary and participative.

To evoke elements from Manukau's own culture, many different materials were textured and molded together, creating abstract designs with motifs from the Pacific, like hibiscus and fisherman's nets. In treating the surface, special relevance was conceded to grass; its green color was counteracted with the warm textures of wood, clay and red volcanic rock. On the clay floor, geometric shapes have been insinuated to evoke nautical charts, while the grassy area is crossed by diagonal paths that connect with the main paths. The wood and Murasaki granite are used to dress the platforms, the sides of which have been made of flagstone to protect against skaters and skateboarders.

The common identity underlying this rich diversity was accentuated by the planting of species like dracaenas,iron trees, the New Zealand Christmas tree, the bird of paradise and harakeke or the sword lily, which are used to manufacture their typical mats. The project achieves a combination, in the same space, of the innovative and the unexpected with the familiar and identifiable. Proof of this is that the community uses this place for celebrating public events as well as for informal activities of a different stripe.

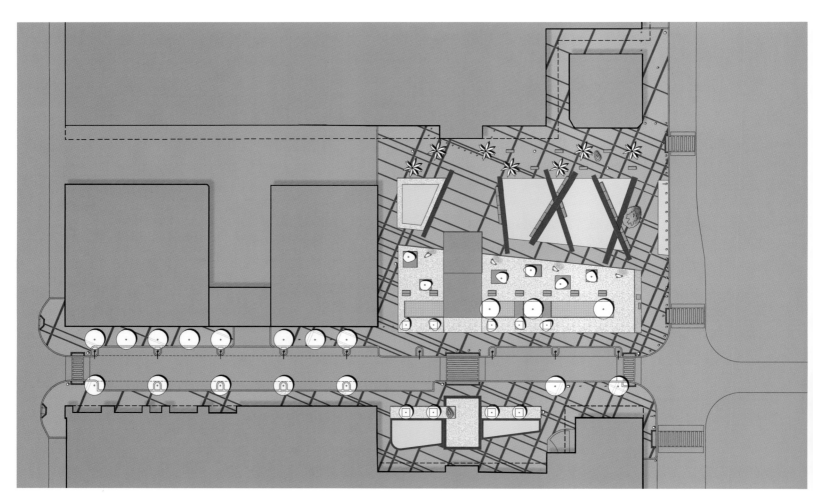

Plan

Elevation

Enclosed Non-Residential Spaces

Gardens

Courtyards

01   Forest Gallery
Carlton Gardens, Victoria, Australia

02   General Mills Corporate Campus
Golden Valley, MN, USA

03   Katharina Sulzer Platz
Winterthur, Switzerland

04   Cour Bleue
Montréal, Canada

05   The Centre for Ideas
Melbourne, Australia

● 01 - 05

Photo © Ben Wrigley, Carla Gottgens

Forest Gallery

Carlton Gardens, Victoria, Australia   2000

LANDSCAPE ARCHITECTS
Taylor Cullity Lethlean

CLIENT
Museum of Victoria

PARTNERS
Kevin Taylor, Perry Lethlean, Ross Privatelli, Damian Schultz, Gini Lee, Mel Speakman, Ben Akerman (principal consultant team); Paul Thompson (planting design); Convergence (exhibition); Arups (structural engineering)

AREA
13,455 SF

COST
2,044,400 euros

What at first seems like a natural forest is, in reality, a garden built into the interior of the new museum center in Melbourne, in a patio that measures 164 by 82 feet. Surrounded on three sides by the building and partially covered by a parallel beam structure, this unique space is the result of collaboration between various professional teams. The garden functions as a space for contemplation for visitors of any age while serving as a reference of the young institution, an open-air museum piece.

Inspiration comes from the forest that covers the mountains near the city: the idea is to capture the essential characteristics of that natural environment, with its flora and fauna, and reconstruct it within the city. The fragment of forest within the rectangular terrain is presented as a densely populated patch of trees, combining different elements of shape, materials and texture; it's a hybrid space, a living sculpture, where the natural and the artificial coexist to shape an abstract landscape. To provide a museum experience

with such peculiar connotations, the garden's design planned for the presence of natural elements that would include specific vegetation, animals, water and an adequate microclimate along with digital technology and other diverse materials. The paths insinuate themselves throughout dense vegetation and pass through little streams until reaching five areas, each representing the causes behind forest changes: water, earth, climate, man and fire.

As an example, human presence leaves behind its traces in the eucalyptus forest, which is transformed into a series of wooden sticks that explain, each and every one, a history related to the forest and its perception. Much like man, fire also leaves its own traces. Some marks made in the ground have been charred and from within the ashes new vegetation is growing. Information regarding the regeneration of the forest after a bushfire is given through an audio system of the latest technology.

Inside the museum patio, a recreation has been made of a fragment of the forest that covers the mountains near Melbourne. The space is conceived as a living sculpture made of vegetation, natural and synthetic materials and digital technology. Visitors may gain admittance to an installation space that evokes the effects of human presence in this environment.

Rendered Plan

Rendered Elevation

Photo © George Heinrich

General Mills Corporate Campus

Golden Valley, MN, USA   2004

LANDSCAPE ARCHITECTS
Oslund & Associates

CLIENT
General Mills

PARTNERS
Tom Oslund, Tadd Kreun (design); HGA Inc (architecture); Commercial Aquatic (water feature)

AREA
34 acres

COST
3,411,600 euros

This corporate campus was built in the 1950s, completed by Skidmore, Owings & Merrill. Acquired by a new business company, the complex needed an enlargement of its entire constructed surface and, as a consequence, of its parking lot as well. The open spaces surrounding new and old buildings alike were subjected to a radical rehabilitation project. The client's principal desire was to create courtyards where employees could enjoy nature and interact with each other during pauses from work or corporate meetings. At the same time, the views from the offices would look out upon a pleasant and picturesque landscape. The generating idea was to create the illusion that the group of buildings were floating within this landscape while brushing against an unmoving mirror of water.

Taking advantage of the slightly undulated profile of the terrain and its groves, the project defines two separate but continuous areas. The first is where the buildings and roads, the primarily functional spaces, are located. The pedestrian walkways that connect the parking lots with the office buildings are outlined by a manipulation of plants and terrain: the main route is bordered by a row of maple trees that culminates in a small forest of lime trees beside the main entrance to the office building.

The interior patios, divided into two levels, and the areas immediately beside the buildings were all renovated with the same common language of shapes and materials; these become functional in accord with the demands of the new property. The surface in these areas is covered by plants and irises in regular strips, slabs of local sandstone, carpets of grass and water that travels in canals from the pond to the pools. The view from these buildings looks out upon a more informal landscape dotted with sculptures.

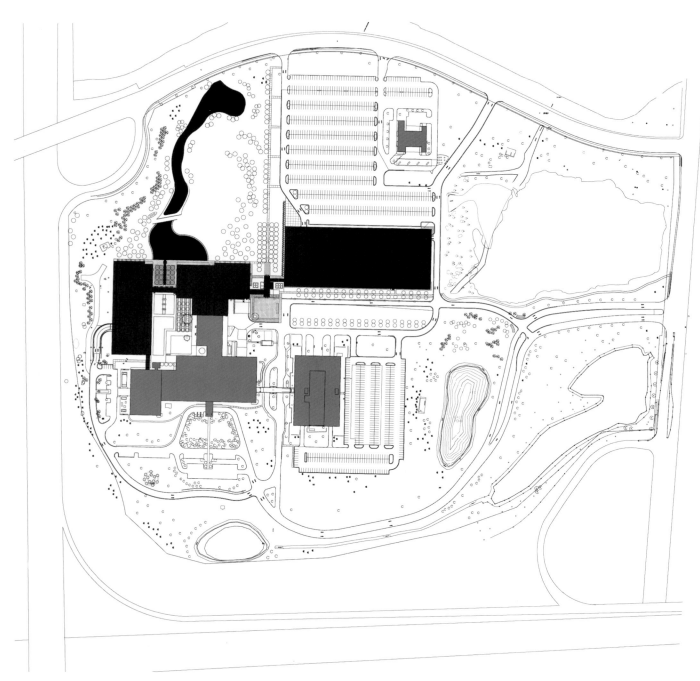

Small stainless steel bridges, similar to the material used in the building's façade, allow for access over the canal that empties into the irregularly-shaped pond. The outside terrace surface is laid with slabs of gray sandstone.

Plan

Photo © Ralph Feiner

Katharina Sulzer Platz

Winterthur, Switzerland   2004

LANDSCAPE ARCHITECTS
Vetsch Nipkow Partner Landschaftsarchitekten

CLIENT
Sulzer Immobilien AG

PARTNERS
Vogt & Partner, Lichgestaltende Ingenieure (consultants); Zschokke (general contractor)

AREA
107,639 SF

COST
3,120,700 euros

The transformation process of the industrial neighborhood in the city of Winterthur, in Switzerland, can be compared with that of other European cities though, in this case, its Helvetian panorama is particularly interesting. The transformation began thanks to urban planning on the part of the local government in 1995, which called for a definitive redevelopment. The singularity of these spaces, characterized by a vast industrial fabric full of large scale buildings, was not to be erased, in fact, the opposite was sought, it would be recognized and taken new advantage of by endowing it with new sense and function. It was also fundamental to create a connection between this area and the adjacent neighborhoods.

Those behind the redevelopment of the Sulzer industrial site's two open areas thought it important to maintain the atmosphere of the place and respect its symbolism. Hence, the intervention's conservation of aesthetics and the simple addition of a few sensibly chosen elements. The transition is made from the industrial to a concept of design. The complexity is in the topographical manipulation of the terrain, where even atmospheric elements play a crucial role. The Katharina Sulzer area is a square and Pionerpark is a type of long patio; in each, the dimensions are vast and the buildings that surround them are converted industrial factories.

The plaza is organized as a visually uniform location while still remaining susceptible to change; the roughness of the chosen surface and its uniform color will change over time to acquire a corrosive aspect. Pionerpark is more of an introverted space, long and narrow, that functions as a connection to other points in the neighborhood. The pavement's design relates to the distinct areas of the park, which are neither static nor unchangeable.

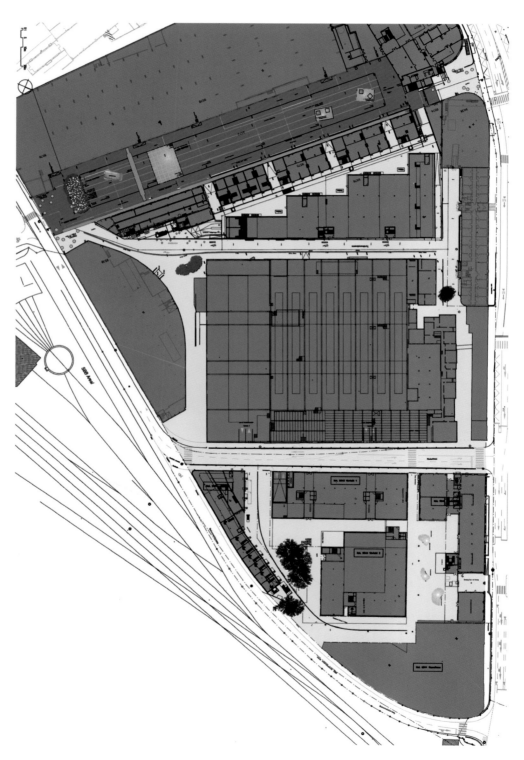

Pionerpark is transformed into a dynamic space that connects with other open spaces in the neighborhood; the old red rail acts as a thread that leads the way through the location. In the patio, the floor is designed with areas that appear random; some of these fill with rain water, frequently becoming mirrors of water.

Site Plan

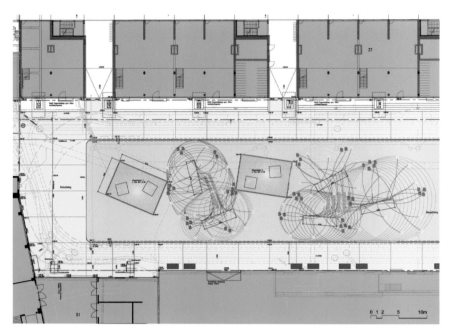

Plan Detail

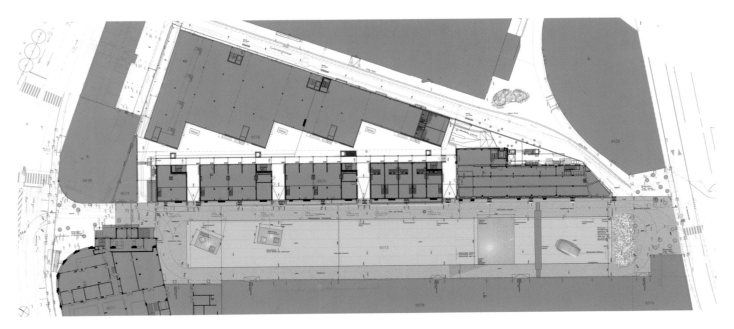

General Plan of the Square

The design of Katharina Sulzer Platz is based on the use of different materials and surfaces to create a uniform area. Use was made of some industrial structures and material, which delineate the different parts of the square. A small patch of trees constitutes the only organic element present.

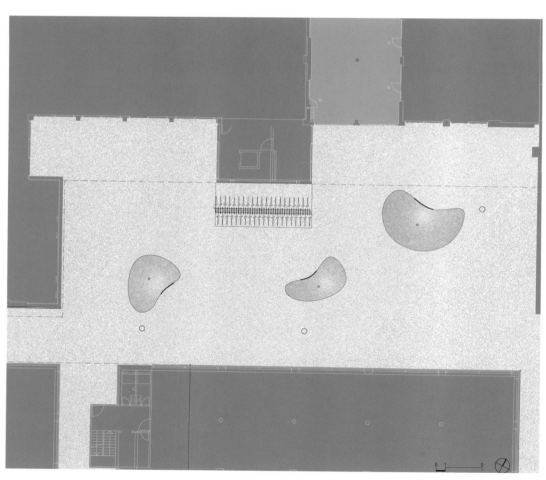

Square Plan

Photo © NIP Paysage

Cour Bleue

Montreal, Canada   2007

LANDSCAPE ARCHITECTS
NIP Paysage

CLIENT
Paul Bruchési School

PARTNERS
*Mini Excavation Beloeil (general contractor);
Annie Ypperciel*

AREA
21,528 SF

COST
68,300 euros

In Montreal, Canada the redevelopment of the playground of the Paul Bruchési elementary school provides an opportunity for playful landscape gestures. The school is in a medium density urban neighborhood, fairly close to the center, characterized by low-rise row houses and mature street trees. A church sits directly across an alley from the schoolyard.

While the typical requirements of a schoolyard with its various athletic courts would not seem to be a brief that is ripe for an inventive landscape design, the designers here have created a landscape with quite an impact. The deployment of colored patterns is used to organize and structure the different uses and programmed activities into zones. A central zone and the areas closer to the school building are reserved for the athletic courts, while the perimeter and far corners lend themselves to more informal uses. The white lines establish a matrix, laying out a backdrop at the scale of the entire schoolyard. These outlines are generated off of the architectural elements on the site, such as

the school's entrances and the building's overall footprint. Sets of double white lines originate at the entrances and extend across the yard, framing the main athletic courts. The game surfaces are inserted into this matrix, along with other elements such as circulation zones. The matrix, more regular and rectilinear in the area of the athletic courts, splinters into a more organic form towards the margins. This net of white lines with ice-blue surfaces becomes an abstract texture of play across the entire yard, giving renewed identity to the generic bituminous material seen in schoolyards everywhere.

Apart from the formal sports courts more playful elements animate the yard. The surface is mounded up into a multifaceted hillock of diversely colored planes of recycled rubber pavement. A variety of trees along with a sprinkling of boulders punctuate the pavement. The boulders double as informal seating. A visually striking grid of dots in the pavement recalls the half-tone printing of children's comic books.

A boulder interrupts the half-tone grid of dots, a resting place for little legs that have run out of steam. Shade trees punctuate the pavement amongst the boulders. The hillock paved in multi-colored recycled rubber rises in a far corner of the schoolyard.

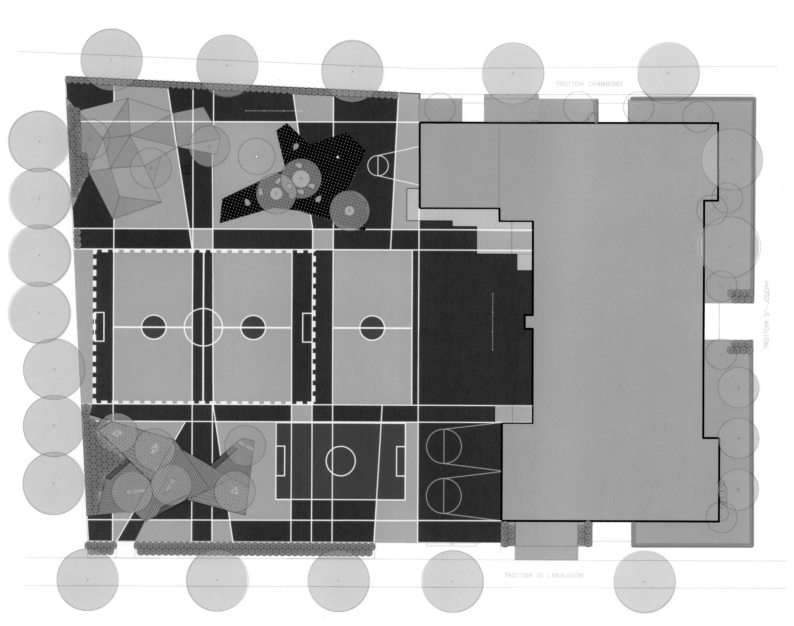

Plan

Photo © Peter Bennetts, Derek Swalwell

The Centre for Ideas

Melbourne, Australia   2003

LANDSCAPE ARCHITECTS
Rush & Wright Associates

CLIENT
Victorian College of the Arts

PARTNERS
Minifie Nixon Architects (constructor)

AREA
6,275 SF

The Victorian College of the Arts is Australia's principal academic institution with regards to the applied visual arts. Since 2007, it has been part of the University of Melbourne, and the building for the recently created Centre for Ideas has become famous for its unique three-dimensional façade of stainless steel panels. In 2004 this project won a landscape award. The intervention confronts the attractive façade and dares to dialogue with it without ceding all attention to the façade. Neither neutral nor modest, the design is based on a geometrically strong and formal landscape schematic that plays with color contrast and other differentiations. Not as rigorous as the building's architectural language, the surrounding area is perceived as a complement that gives the entire complex an almost surrealist atmosphere.

The geometry was inspired on the text *Order in Space*, by Keith Critchlow, a classic that offers a unique look into the meeting point between mathematics and art, which is useful come time to confront themes such as the definition of a space. The chosen shapes are not casual, but derive from the hexagon. Sophisticated geometries, variations in surface and color usage all translate into one complex project. The surface, paved in black and white strips of cement and asphalt, is converted, at its extremes, into a group of polygons in shades of white and gray, except for the blue staircase steps. The vegetation chosen pertains to the type of robust native species that doesn't shy away from high temperatures, while some Australian pines will eventually grow to provide an important complement to the building within a few years.

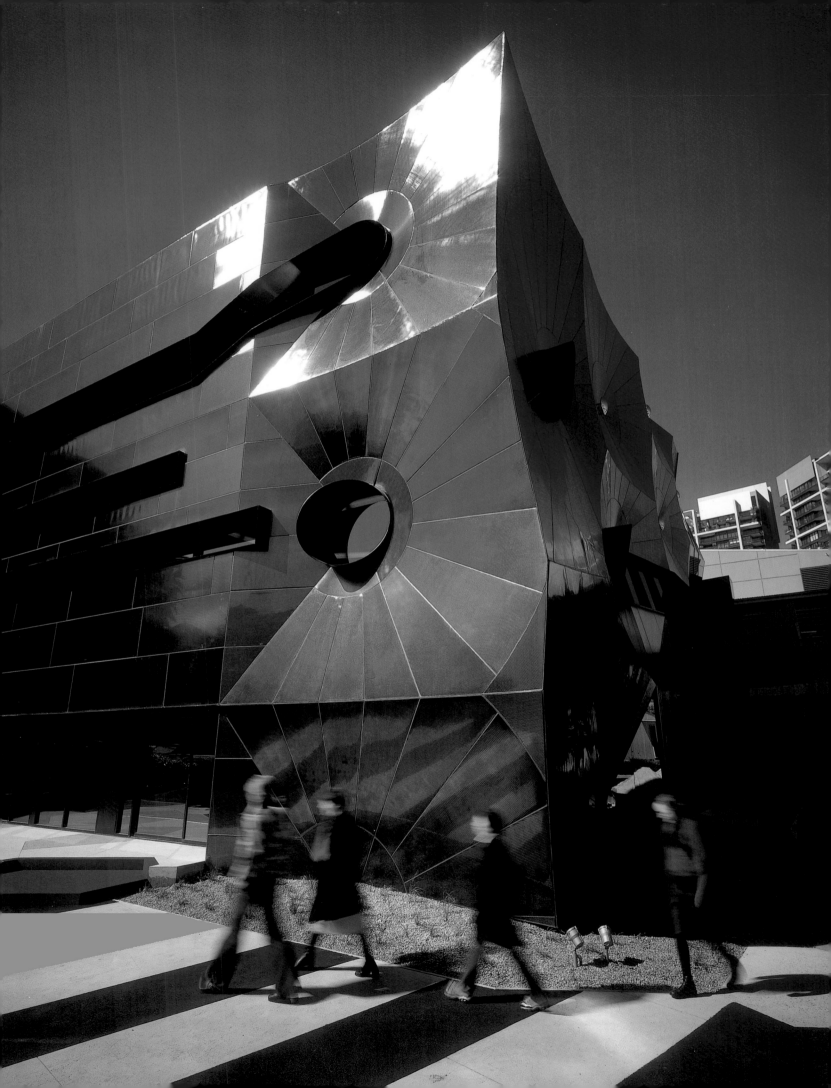

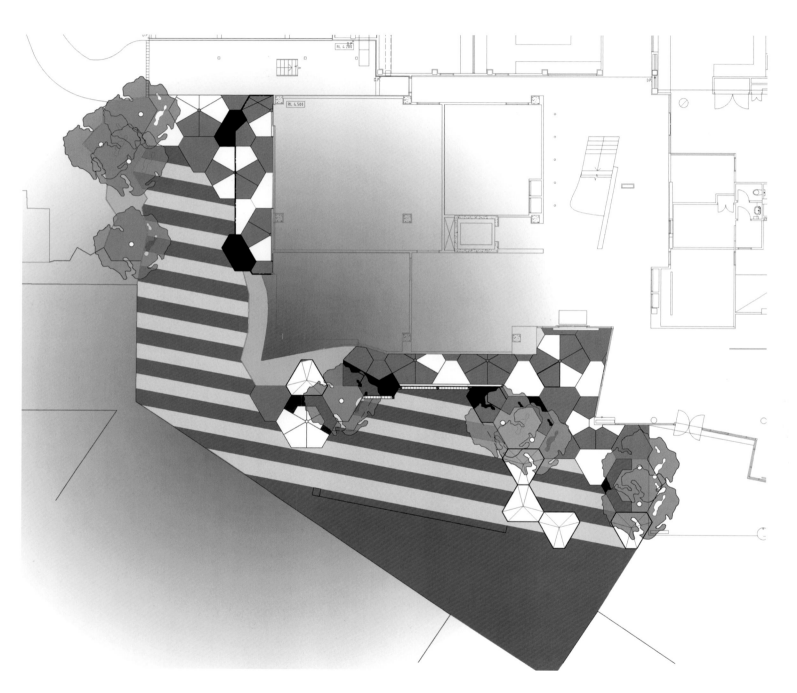

Corresponding with the building's entryways, the black and white strips become white and gray hexagons. Among the composition's elements, small mounds of artificial material rise from the ground in the shape of pyramids.

Plan

3D Rendering

Residential Spaces

Gardens

Courtyards

Green Roofs

01   Las Margas Parks and Gardens
Latas, Spain

02   Organic Farming Garden
Sant Cristòfol, Spain

03   Court Square Press Courtyard Garden
Boston, MA, USA

04   Danse en Ligne
Montreal, Canada

05   Charlotte Garden
Copenhagen, Denmark

06   151 East Jaques Avenue
Bondi, Australia

07   Unterföhring Park Village
Unterföhring, Germany

Photo © Verzone Woods Architectes, Nozar SA

Las Margas Parks and Gardens

Latas, Spain   2007

LANDSCAPE ARCHITECTS
Verzone Woods Architectes

CLIENT
City Council of Latas

PARTNERS
Craig Verzone, Cristina Woods, Martin Gauthier, Robert de Miguel, Vera Baptista, Frédéric Duperray, Nicole Graber, DAN Hallstrom, Thomas Dromelet (design team); Ruiz Lacruz Arquitectos & Abadias Arquitecto (architecture); ATAIN SA (engineering); Nozar SA (development)

AREA
395.5 acres

Situated at the foot of the Pyrenees mountains in the far north of the Spanish province of Aragon, near the town of Sabiñánigo, this project proposes an ambitious program of twenty-two hundred units of housing, golf courses (twenty-seven holes), a club house and hotel, commercial spaces, schools, social centers and nearly 200 acres of nature reserve, public parks and private gardens. Phase one, recently completed, includes the golf courses, clubhouse and hotel, two hundred fifty units of housing, the core zones of public space, private gardens and a semi-public swimming and sports complex.

Given the importance of the region's natural resources and rich vernacular architectural language, the project grew from the design team's initial ecological and architectural studies of the surrounding area and landscape. A series of new artificial lagoons, public promenades and fingers of parkland will play an important role in connecting the residents to the plethora of outdoor activities that already exits in the surrounding Tena Valley.

The main public park area adjacent to the clubhouse is a series of lagoons that spill one into the next. The highly articulated, terraced surface of the parks are painted, as if abstract canvases, with a rich variety of paving materials: several different kinds of wood decking, rounded river rocks, abstractly patterned concrete, smooth poured concrete, flagstone, grass and gravel. Retaining walls are constructed variously of steel plate or finished in stone.

The sheet steel walls result in a crisp knife-edge at the top. Landscape steps are also formed of the same steel plate detail. A forest of highly adaptable, abstract light standards populates the landscape. At times they can be simple straight posts projecting out of the ground at a skewed angle or alternatively they sprout a long arm that reaches over a path, or they morph into the structure of a bench and sheltering trelliswork. Variety is also found in the species of trees used, from pines to cypresses to various broad-leafed trees.

A rich and contrasting variety of materials and pavements intersect. As viewed from above in plan, they have a painterly effect. From the ground level viewpoint of a stroller, the crisp details offer a constantly changing visual interest, set off by the backdrop of dark green rolling foothills beyond

Site Plan

Photo © Adrià Goula

Organic Farming Garden

Sant Cristòfol, Spain   2006

LANDSCAPE ARCHITECTS
*Claudi Aguiló/Data AE Arquitectura i
Enginyeria*

CLIENT
private

PARTNERS
*Emma Martí (architect); Elena Mostazo
(agronomist); Lauric Construccions i Reformes
(constructor)*

AREA
8,460 SF

COST
120,200 euros

This garden is in a rural area about 25 miles northwest of Barcelona at the village of Sant Cristòfol. The context is a landscape of detached houses and small scale agriculture on rolling terrain. It is in the shadow of Montserrat, a spectacular mountain range of up-thrusting stone mounds which lies just a mile or so to the south. The garden is organized on a steeply sloping plot of private land between the main house and a guest cottage. It is intended to both produce organically grown fruits and vegetables and to be enjoyed as a landscape or ornamental garden. Considerable production of produce is expected from intensive organic cultivation techniques.

To achieve this, the site has been terraced with reinforced concrete retaining walls. A rustic feel is imparted to the bare walls by board-forming the concrete and staining it with a rust tint. While the majority of the area is dedicated to cultivating food plants, the margins are planted with bushes and native shrubs that are easily maintained and require little water. The uppermost terrace

level is turned over primarily to lawn and serves as a perch from which one may enjoy the views, both long views across the rural terrain and intimate views of the organic garden as it spills down the slope. The middle terrace grows a combination of fruit trees and seasonal vegetables while the lowest level along the street is primarily fruit trees.

The linearity of the space is emphasized by the tall retaining walls and the multiple parallel paths between the two buildings. Paving for the paths is accomplished through the use of pre-fabricated paving elements that rest lightly on the soil without interfering with absorption of rainwater or the subsurface water flows. They allow guests to enjoy a walk through the garden without compacting the soil too much. The terraces and paths end abruptly at one end where steep steps next to an ivy-choked garden wall connect the levels. At the other end the terraces spill out in more gradual planes canted towards the guest house.

From the uppermost terrace, views both long and short may be enjoyed.
Here we see the countryside as it slopes gradually off into the distance.
Steep connecting stairs of site-formed concrete descend one edge of the
garden. Native shrubs and herbs can be seen along the side of the steps.

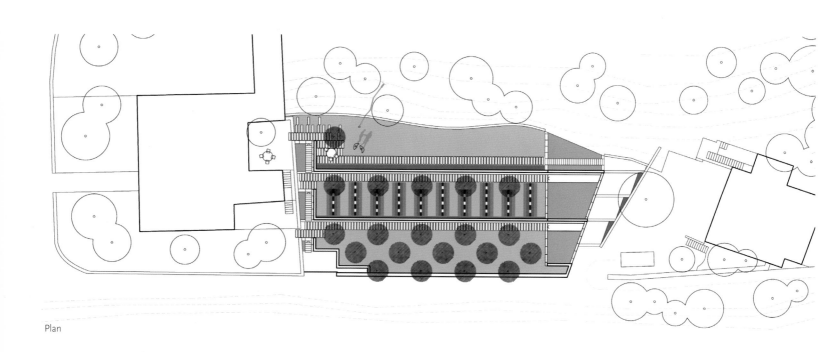

Plan

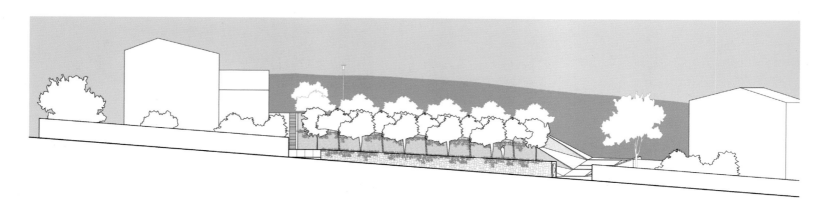

Elevation

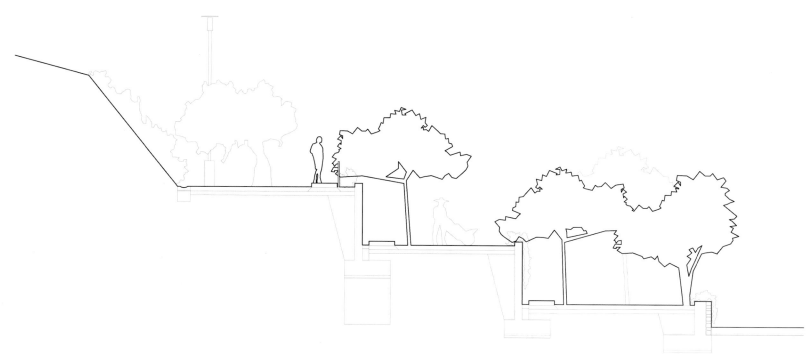

Section

Photomontage

Vines spill over the rust-stained reinforced concrete walls. These walls bear the texture of board-forming that gives them the look of layers of soil, while their tint reflects the red earth color of the soil. The path is laid out with pre-fabricated blocks placed lightly on the soil, allowing for drainage and minimizing soil compaction.

Photo © Landworks Studio

Court Square Garden

Boston, MA, USA   2003

LANDSCAPE ARCHITECTS
John Cunningham Architects, Landworks Studio, Office DA

CLIENT
Private

PARTNERS
A. J. Martini (general contractor); Emanouil Brothers Inc (landscape contractor); D. M. Berg Consultants (structural engineer); Pappas Enterprises Inc (developer)

AREA
210,000 SF (site)

The Court Square Press Building is in the waterfront Fort Point Channel neighborhood of Boston, Massachusetts. The surrounding urban context is characterized by asphalt parking lots, cobble strewn tracts, and the remnants of abandoned railroad yards. The building itself is a massive, 19th century brick industrial structure that has been renovated into residential units.

The building's renovation left open a courtyard space which inspired the developer with a vision of a common green area. The goal for the design was to create a private oasis for the residents in this otherwise gritty urban context. The idea of fragmentation is generative for this scheme, as each window looks out upon just a fragment of the garden, and privacy needs call for a thick canopy of vegetation to block views directly across the courtyard.

A deck/walkway structure built of alternating sections of ipe wood and aluminum panels traverses the space in a fragmented form that is punctuated by internally-lit benches. The benches appear scattered about but are carefully placed in small clearings in the

bamboo forest and away from bedroom windows and more private interior spaces. Similar to a camp fire experience, people gather around the illuminated benches to converse, tell stories, and linger in the forest.

Lighting, both natural and artificial, play a central role in the design concept. The courtyard is quite deep as it is surrounded by an unrelenting, six-story high grid of windows puncturing the massive brick walls. Because of the courtyard's east-west orientation, indirect sunlight reflects off these windows to illuminate the courtyard floor. While artificial light from the colored, light-box benches provides path lighting, higher up a proposed forest of yellow fiber optic lines will mimic the bamboo stalks. These will be connected at the cornice level to a network of stainless steel cables. As the garden matures it will visually separate opposing residences. By day the supporting web of cables will be visible as an interesting complex of lines casting shadows in the treetops. By night the cables will recede into the shadows as the thicket of linear lights emerge, floating in the bamboo.

Fragmented shards of alternating ipe wood and aluminum panels form the thin deck surface that floats above the undulating ground surface. Plantings are placed to block direct views into private ground level windows. Not yet installed are the fiber optic light lines and stainless steel cable canopy.

Section

Perspective

Photo © NIP Paysage

Danse en Ligne

Montreal, Canada   2007

LANDSCAPE ARCHITECTS
NIP Paysage

CLIENT
Les Développements D'arcy McGee Ltée

PARTNERS
Frederico Bizotto, Carlo Bizzotto, Patrick Morand, Carl Tremblay (consultants); Les Développements D'arcy McGee Ltée (general contractor)

AREA
7,535 SF

This garden courtyard, in a residential project in Montreal, Canada, spans the discrepancies between an old industrial building (re-used for residential units) and a newly-built condominium building. The project is located in a formerly industrial zone close to the city center.

The courtyard sits on the roof of a subterranean parking garage, which limits the extent of the plantings.

The animating essence of the design is the scale and texture of the large, flat expanse of cedar decking with its subtle canting in the direction that the boards are laid. This is done in response to the two mismatched façades. Wedge-shaped sections fan out alternately from one or the other facades giving the perfectly level expanse the look of tilted planes: a topography where none actually exists. The extensive use of wood is to achieve a contrast that distinguishes it from the generally mineral ambiance of the surrounding central-city urban fabric.

Minimal and discrete are the elements placed upon, and puncturing, this plane of wood, creating a spare, syncopated rhythm across the space. The wedge shapes of the decking are repeated again in planters and stair structures that march across the facades of the buildings, each slightly different than the next but all of the same part: wood steps climbing up the side of a wood planter stripped open at the front end exposing its gravel filling like a terrarium. The wedge (or trapezoid) shape is again used in forming a series of super-minimalist gazebos. These structures define volumes with the absolute minimum expression: just the lines that draw the edges of a box volume. Another note in this syncopated rhythm is the slots cut into the deck, filled with gravel and planted with ivy.

The traditional role of the courtyard as a meeting place for the surrounding buildings is reinforced here with the front stoops that address the space directly, and the ample provision of a variety of seating areas, including bright green plastic pods and wooden chaise lounges.

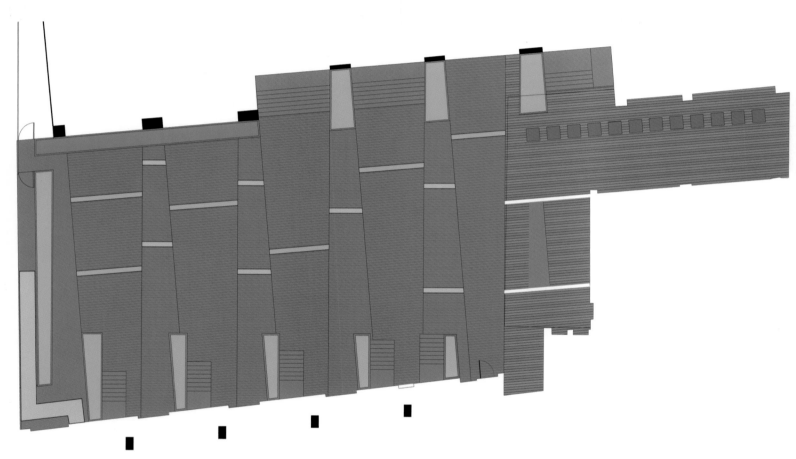

Plan

Photo © Torben Petersen

Charlotte Garden

Copenhagen, Denmark   2004

LANDSCAPE ARCHITECTS
SLA

CLIENT
Harald Simonsens Ejendomsselskab

PARTNERS
Stig L. Andersson (creative director); Hanne Brunn Møller (project manager); Lars Nybye Sørensen, Lundgaard & Tranberg Architects, Hansen & Henneberg Lighting Engineers, Hampus Naturleg (others)

AREA
26,910 SF

COST
1,080,000 euros

Charlottehaven is a residential complex with about two hundred units, situated on Strandboulevard, an avenue close to the Nordhavn station in Copenhagen. The garden is located in the middle of a typical community patio and surrounded by housing blocks on all four sides. In turn, the use of this space is primarily neighborhood-related, a local population that uses the space for socializing, meeting, rest and play.

The landscaper's original desire was to bring nature straight into the city, in this case to the interior of the block, so that the neighbors could see it and breathe it each time they looked out their windows. But, for the project's architect, the idea of nature in an urban space could not be translated into something concrete, but something changing: the shape and color of the plants change throughout the year and during the different seasons, offering a different experience each time. In this sense, the double perception enhanced by this project becomes fundamental: one from the apartment windows and another from ground level.

The perspectives change with the observer's point of view. From above, the garden appears to be a dynamic drawing composed of different patches joined by the layout of pedestrian walkways. The garden of vegetable dunes recalls the coastal countryside: the vegetation is primarily composed of perennial greens, like the blue fescue, seslevia and molinia caerulea. These species go from green and blue in the summer to red and yellow tones in the winter. They offer a colorful spectacle that is rare in these latitudes.

Below, at garden level, the experience is multi-sensorial: the richness of the spaces is translated through enjoyment of the smells and colors these plants provide and the sound of the wind. Spaces that involve and offer occasion to rest, take in the sun, play and walk. The paths are lined with iron sides that integrate aesthetically with the changing colors of the vegetation. The garden is seen as a rare experience twenty-four hours a day. At night, delicate red spotlights illuminate the paths and a selection of plants create a setting of emotional impact.

Plan

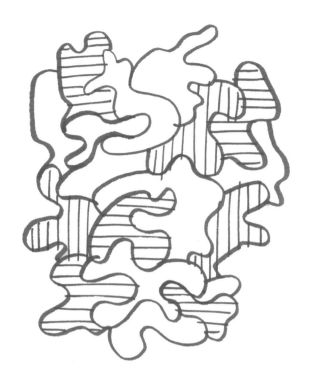

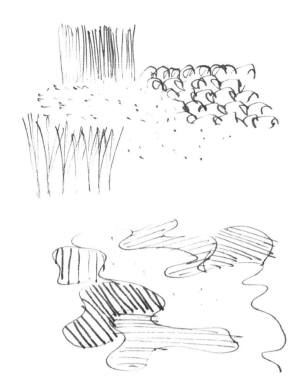

Sketches

Photo © Simon Wood

151 East Jaques Avenue
Bondi, Australia   2005

LANDSCAPE ARCHITECTS
Aspect Studios

CLIENT
private

PARTNERS
Alexander Tzannes Associates

AREA
1,184 SF

COST
312,800 euros

This project is for the design of a central courtyard and grounds of a mid-rise apartment building complex in Bondi, Australia, near central Sydney, and just a block away from the beach at Bondi Bay.

The need was for landscaping in a courtyard that serves as a light well and is a highly visible space, the focus point of the apartment complex. Privacy screening between the flanking rows of apartments was also a concern. While the center of the courtyard is intended as a common green space to be viewed but not entered, the edges are lined with private patios for adjoining the units. The majority of the units in the complex look in on this courtyard. Additional landscaping was planned at the street facades of the complex.

The central feature of the courtyard sits atop a raised podium. Borrowing from the Bondi Bay beach just a short distance away, this part of the design is based upon the lines and layers carved by the wash of the surf on the shoreline. A series of irregular parallel strips that contain feature plantings and

materials are intended to be experienced both from the balconies above and at ground level. The strips are filled variously with water, endemic native costal plants, and local rocks or crushed gravel. The planting is designed to create privacy between the facing rows of apartments while allowing in light and air. A large three-story opening in the building facade provides a framed view into the courtyard from the street.

At the individual patios privacy is provided through a variety of screening devices. Bamboo and native trees are used, as well as plexiglas and latticework screens. Steel frames have been installed for climbing vines to act as a further privacy measure. All of this screening is not so much that it takes away from the expansiveness of these outdoor rooms. Finely crafted wood fences round out the palette of materials.

The existing street trees along the street facades have been supplemented by the addition of paperbarks, a species of tree native to Australia.

Loosely parallel strips constructed in concrete contain a palette of native materials. The water course is underlain with rounded local rocks. White gravel contrasts with the plantings. The plants are all species indigenous to the nearby Australian coast. The effect is equally impressive whether viewed from above in plan, or at ground level.

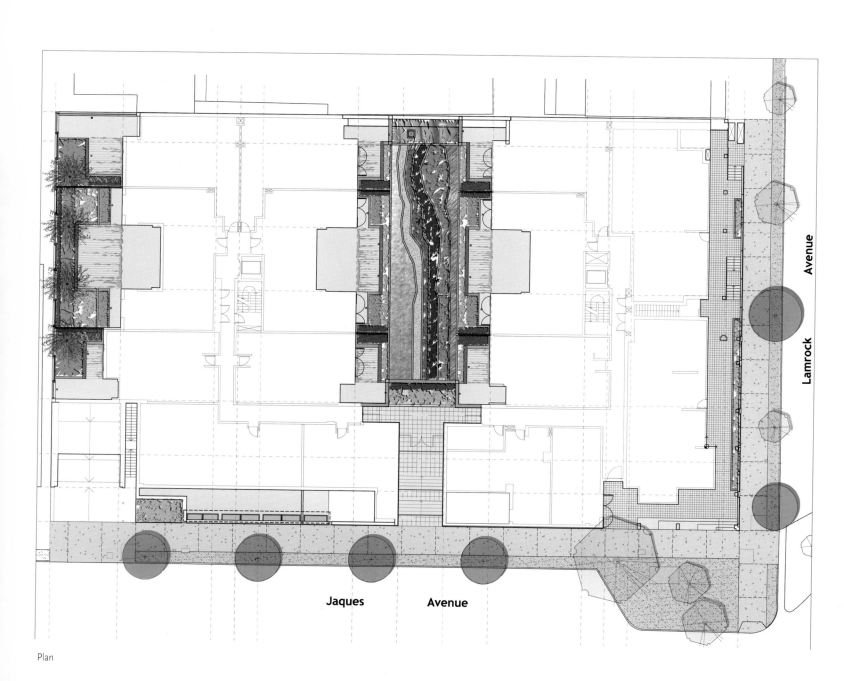

Lamrock Avenue

Jaques Avenue

Plan

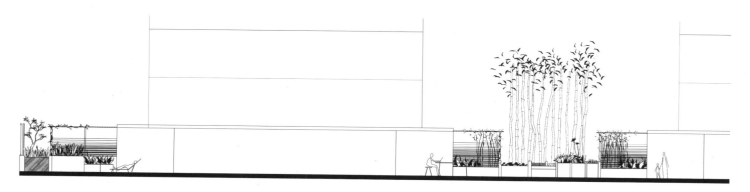

Elevation

Photo © Florian Holzherr, Burger Landschaftsarchitekten, Rakete

Unterföhring Park Village

Unterföhring, Germany   2003

LANDSCAPE ARCHITECTS
Burger Landschaftsarchitekten

CLIENT
Merkur GmbH & Co, Objekt Unterföhring KG

PARTNERS
MVRDV Lauber Architekten, BGSP&K (architects)

AREA
4.4 acres

COST
1,700,000 euros

Unterföhring is the most extensive neighborhood devoted to the service sector in Munich. Located halfway between the center of the city and the airport, the area has witnessed the arrival of many new company headquarters in recent years. In this neighborhood's fragmented fabric, the Dutch team MVRDV has created a master plan out of a group of buildings that form a dense urban structure. Arranged according to a Cartesian coordinate system, the nineteen rectangular blocks of diverse size are characterized by their different facades, heights, colors and materials.

This small village proposes itself as an open space that creates a compact and uniform urban fabric. The task of conferring certain uniformity to the whole was assumed into the project. Under the premise of finding variety in unity, the design centers on two different levels: the first is on a street-level while the second refers to the rooftops themselves. The spaces between the buildings provide a unifying element; slabs of gray stone used for the floor's surface. In exchange, the rooftops are covered with col-

orful gardens that vary from building to building to emphasize the independent character of each block. The rigid and orthogonal design of the urban fabric contrasts with the irregularly-shaped slabs of stone, which are arranged in a continuous shape with respect to the central pathways but joined with various sized patches of green along the sides. There is no furniture or seating to occupy space. Lighting comes from the office windows until late at night, and three lamps are located in the cafeteria area.

The gardened rooftops, few of which are actually accessible, have an individual design characterized by carpets of vegetation that vary in color depending on the essences used: yellow sedum, blue grasses, violet lavenders, field flowers, etcetera. The roof of the building that holds the bar is the only one adorned with slabs of stone and Irish moss. The design is centered by a clear definition of shapes, highlighted by the use of attractive materials and careful details.

Plan

Agence APS Paysagistes DPLG Associés
31 Grande-rue
26000 Valence, France
Tel.: + 33 04 75 78 53 53
Fax: + 33 04 75 78 53 50
www.agenceaps.com
Aristide Briand Square

AllesWirdGut Architektur
Josefstädter Strasse 74, top B
1080 Wien, Austria
Tel.: + 43 1 96 10 437 0
Fax: + 43 1 96 40 437 11
www.alleswirdgut.cc
Pedestrian Area FUZI

Arriola & Fiol Arquitectes
Mallorca 289
08037 Barcelona, Spain
Tel.: + 34 93 457 03 57
Fax: + 34 93 208 04 59
www.arriolafiol.com
Central Park of Nou Barris and Virrei Amat Square

Arpas Arquitectos Paisagistas Associados
Av. 24 Julho 92, 2E
1200-870 Lisboa, Portugal
Tel.: + 35 213 97 90 54
Fax: + 35 213 97 90 53
City Park of Beja

Ashton Raggatt McDougall Architects
522 Finders Lane, level 11
3000 Melbourne, Australia
Tel.: + 61 03 9629 1222
Fax: + 61 03 9629 4220
www.a-r-m.com.au
Grand Plaza

Aspect Studios
Studio 61, level 6
61 Marlborough Street, Surry Hills
2010 NSW, Sydney, Australia
Tel.: + 61 02 9699 7182
Fax: + 61 02 9699 7192
www.aspect.net.au
151 East Jaques Avenue

BB & GG Arquitectes
Passatge Escudellers 5, baixos
08002 Barcelona, Spain
Tel.: + 34 93 412 68 78
Fax: + 34 93 412 64 57
www.bethgali.com
Remodeling of Joan Miró Park
Zona de Banys Fòrum

Burckhardt & Partner Architekten
Neumarkt 28
8022 Zurich, Switzerland
Tel.: + 41 44 262 36 46
Fax: + 41 44 262 32 74
www.burckhardtpartner.ch
MFO Park

Burger Landschaftsarchitekten
Rosenheimer Straße 139
81671 Munich, Germany
Tel.: + 49 89 49 000 925
Fax: + 49 89 49 000 926
www.burgerlandschaftsarchitekten.de
Green Axis 13
Unterföhring Park Village

Carlos Martínez Architekten
Sonnenstrasse 8B
CH-9443 Widnau, Switzerland
Tel.: + 41 71 727 99 55
Fax: + 41 71 727 99 44
www.carlosmartinez.ch
Stadtlounge St. Gallen

Carl-Viggo Hølmebakk
Sofiesgate 70
0168 Oslo, Norway
Tel.: + 47 22 46 76 00
Fax: + 47 22 46 76 00
Sohlbergplassen Viewpoint

Christopher Kelly/Architecture Workshop
PO BOX 9572, Wellington, New Zealand
Tel.: + 64 04 473 44 38
Fax: + 64 04 473 95 72
www.archwksp.co.nz
Oriental Bay Enhancement

Claude Cormier Architectes Paysagistes
5600, De Normanville
H2S 2B2 Montreal, Quebec, Canada
Tel.: + 1 514 849 8262
Fax: + 1 514 279 8076
www.claudecormier.com
HTO
Solange

Claudi Aguiló/Data AE Arquitectura i Enginyeria
Bailén 28, 2°-1ª
08010 Barcelona, Spain
Tel.: + 34 93 265 19 47
Fax: + 34 93 265 61 26
www.dataae.com
Organic Farming Garden

CS&P Architects
2345 Yonge Street, suite 200
M4P 235 Toronto, Ontario, Canada
Tel.: + 1 416 482 5002
Fax: + 1 416 482 5040
www.csparch.com
Welland Canal

Dal Pian Arquitetos
Av. Higienópolis 529, cj. 11
CEP 01238 001 São Paulo, Brazil
Tel.: + 55 11 3822 1218
Fax: + 55 11 3822 5186
www.dalpian.arq.br
Das Águas Square

David Chipperfield Architects
Cobham Mews
Agar Grove, Camden
NW1 9SB London, United Kingdom
Tel.: + 44 0 207 267 9422
Fax: + 44 0 207 267 9347
www.davidchipperfield.co.uk
Teruel Urban Development

David Irwin/Isthmus Group
43 Sale Street, Freemans Bay
PO Box 90 366, Auckland, New Zealand
Tel.: + 64 09 309 9442
Fax: + 64 09 309 9060
www.isthmus.co.nz
Manukau Square
Oriental Bay Enhancement

De Amicis Architetti
Via Pietrasanta 12
20141 Milano, Italy
Tel.: + 39 02 55 23 16 26
Fax: + 39 02 57 41 92 07
www.deamicisarchitetti.it
Incontro Tra i Popoli Square

Donaldson & Warm Architects
38 Roe Street
6000 Perth, Western Australia
Tel.: + 61 08 9328 4475
Fax: + 61 08 9227 6558
www.donaldsonandwarn.com.au
Bali Memorial

EDAW
150 Chestnut Street
94111 San Francisco, CA, USA
Tel.: + 1 415 433 14 84
Fax: + 1 415 788 48 75
www.edaw.com
Hai River Embankment Design
Piccadilly Gardens
Royal Victoria Square

Estudio Felipe Peña & Francisco Novoa
San Andrés 138, 1°
15003 A Coruña, Spain
Tel.: + 34 98 122 19 74
Fax: + 34 98 121 79 93
Ethnographic Park

Fermín Vázquez/B720 Arquitectos
Josep Tarradellas 123
08029 Barcelona, Spain
Tel.: + 34 93 363 79 79
Fax: + 34 93 363 01 39
www.b720.com
Teruel Urban Development

François Tribel/Atelier Grunig Tribel
70 ter, allée Darius Milhaud
75 019 Paris, France
Tel.: + 33 01 42 06 55 99
Fax: + 33 01 42 06 77 22
www.grunig-tribel.com
François Mitterrand Square

Germán del Sol
Camino las Flores, 11441
Las Condes, Santiago de Chile, Chile
Tel.: + 56 2 214 1214
Fax: + 56 2 214 1147
www.germandelsol.cl
Termas Geométricas
Termas de Puritama

GORA Art & Landscape
Vilebovägen 4A
SE-21763 Malmö, Sweden
Tel.: + 46 40 911 913
Fax: + 46 40 911 903
www.gora.se
Traffic Junction Odenskog

Grupo de Diseño Urbano
Fernando Montes de Oca 4
06140 Colonia Condesa, DF, Mexico
Tel.: + 52 55 531 248
Fax: + 52 52 861 013
www.gdu.com.mx
Union Point Park

Hariri Pontarini Architects
245 Davenport Road, 3rd floor
M5R 1K1 Toronto, Ontario, Canada
Tel.: + 1 416 929 4901
Fax: + 1 416 929 8924
www.hariripontarini.com
HTO

Hideki Yoshimatsu & Archipro Architects
3-6-16-104 Kitazawa Setagaya
155-0031 Tokyo, Japan
Tel.: + 81 3 5453 5081
Fax: + 81 3 5453 5082
www.archipro.net
Cemetery for the Unknown

Hutterreimann & Cejka Landschaftsarchitekten
Möckernstraße 68
10965 Berlin, Germany
Tel.: + 49 30 78 898 825
Fax: + 49 30 78 095 488
www.hr-c.net
Landesgartenschau Wernigerode 2006

Janet Rosenberg & Associates
148 Kenwood Avenue
M6C 2S3 Toronto, Ontario, Canada
Tel.: + 1 416 656 6665
Fax: + 1 416 656 5756
www.jrala.ca
Harmony of Opposites
HTO
Town Hall Square
Welland Canal

Jensen & Skodvin Arkitektkontor
Fredensborgveien 11
0177 Oslo, Norway
Tel.: + 47 22 99 48 99
Fax: + 47 22 99 48 88
www.jsa.no
Gudbrandsjuvet

Jens Schmahl/A Lab Architektur
Rathausstrasse 7
10178 Berlin, Germany
Tel.: + 49 30 25 294 990
Fax: + 49 30 25 294 991
www.a-lab.net
Landesgartenschau Wernigerode 2006

JML Arquitectura del Agua
Paseo de los Tilos 21
08034 Barcelona, Spain
Tel.: + 34 93 280 53 74
Fax: + 34 93 280 62 44
www.jeanmaxllorca.com
Fira Montjuïc 2 in Barcelona
François Mitterrand Square

John Cunningham Architects
655 Summer Street
02210 Boston, MA, USA
Tel.: + 1 617 951 02 66
Fax: + 1 617 439 94 42
Court Square Garden

Jos van de Lindeloof Tuin en Landschapsarchitectenbureau
Martinus Nijhofflaan 2
2624 ES Delft, The Netherlands
Tel.: + 31 0 15 213 34 44
Fax: + 31 0 15 284 09 17
www.josvandelindeloof.nl
Meerterpen Cemetery

Karres en Brands Landschapsarchitecten
Oude Amersfoortseweg 123
1212 AA Hilversum, The Netherlands
Tel.: + 31 0 35 642 29 62
www.karresenbrands.nl
Berestein Cemetery

Koepfli Partner Landschafsarchitekten
Neustadtstrasse 3
6003 Luzern, Switzerland
Tel.: + 41 41 226 16 46
Fax: + 41 41 226 17 27
www.koeflipartner.ch
Seebad Zweiern

LAND-I Archicolture
Via Madonna dei Monti 50
00184 Roma, Italy
Tel.: + 39 06 47 46 78 2
Fax: + 39 06 23 32 24 110
www.archicolture.com
Mente la-menta?

Landskap Design
Bredsgården 2A, Bryggen
5003 Bergen, Norway
Tel.: + 47 55 56 33 15
Fax: + 47 55 56 33 16
www.landskapdesign.no
Festplassen

Landslag ehf Landslagsarkitektar FÍLA
Skólavörðustíg 11
101 Reykjavík, Iceland
Tel.: + 354 535 53 00
Fax: + 354 535 53 01
www.landslag.is
Avalanche Defense Structures in Iceland
Litlatún

Landworks Studio
355 Congress Street
02210 Boston, MA, USA
Tel.: + 1 617 399 06 57
Fax: + 1 617 399 06 60
www.landworks-studio.com
Court Square Garden

Made Associati Architettura e Paesaggio
Vicolo Pescatori 2
31100 Treviso, Italy
Tel.: + 39 04 22 59 01 98
Fax: + 39 04 22 59 01 98
www.madeassociati.it
Cendon di Silea

McGregor & Partners
21C Wistler Street
2095 NSW, Manly, Sydney, Australia
Tel.: + 61 02 9977 3853
Fax: + 61 02 9976 5501
www.mcgregorpartners.com.au
Amoeba 2

Miró Rivera Architects
505 Powell Street
78703 Austin, TX, USA
Tel.: + 1 512 477 70 16
Fax: + 1 512 476 76 72
www.mirorivera.com
Pedestrian Bridge

Mosbach Paysagistes
81 rue des Poissonniers
75018 Paris, France
Tel.: + 33 01 53 38 49 99
Fax: + 33 01 42 41 22 10
Botanical Garden of Bordeaux

NIP Paysage
7468 Drolet
H2R 2C4 Montreal, Quebec, Canada
Tel.: + 1 514 272 6626
Fax: + 1 514 272 6622
www.nippaysage.ca
Cour Bleue
Danse en Ligne
Impluvium
In Vitro
Trans[plant]

Obras Architectes
42 rue d'Avron
75020 Paris, France
Tel.: + 33 01 43 48 06 92
Fax: + 33 01 43 70 24 30
www.paysages.net
La Ereta Park

Office DA
1920 Washington Street 2
02118 Boston, MA, USA
Tel.: + 1 617 541 55 40
Fax: + 1 617 541 55 35
www.officeda.com
Court Square Garden

Oslund & Associates
115 Washington Ave. N., suite 200
55401 Minneapolis, MN, USA
Tel.: + 1 612 359 91 44
Fax: + 1 612 359 96 25
www.oaala.com
General Mills Corporate Campus

Paolo L. Bürgi
6528 Camorino, Switzerland
Tel.: + 41 91 857 27 29
Fax: + 41 91 857 36 26
www.burgi.ch
Kreuzlingen Hafenplatz

Pierre Lafon
29 rue Saint-Melaine
35000 Rennes, France
Tel.: + 33 06 80 47 63 66
Fax: + 33 02 99 36 26 63
www.pierlafon.net
Remodeling of River Bank

Pipilotti Rist/Hauser & Wirth
Limmatstrasse 270
CH-8005 Zurich, Switzerland
Tel.: + 41 44 446 80 50
Fax: + 41 44 446 80 50
www.pipilottirist.net
Stadtlounge St. Gallen

Proap
Rua Dom Luís I 19, 6ffl
1200-149 Lisboa, Portugal
Tel.: + 351 21 395 17 24
Fax: + 351 21 395 35 20
www.proap.pt
Ourém's Linear Park

PWP Landscape Architecture
739 Allston Way
94710 Berkeley, CA, USA
Tel.: + 1 510 849 94 94
Fax: + 1 510 849 93 33
www.pwpla.com
Kiel Triangle Plaza
Saitama Plaza

Raderschall Landschaftsarchitekten
Burgstrasse 69
8706 Meilen, Switzerland
Tel.: + 41 44 925 55 00
Fax: + 41 44 925 55 01
www.raderschall.ch
MFO Park

Ravetllat & Ribas Arquitectes
Rambla de Catalunya 11, pral. 2°
08007 Barcelona, Spain
Tel.: + 34 93 280 26 90
Fax: + 34 93 280 04 34
Passeig Garcia Fària

RCR Aranda Pigem Vilalta Arquitectes
Passeig Blay 34, 2°
17800 Olot, Spain
Tel.: + 34 97 226 91 05
Fax: + 34 97 226 75 58
www.rcrarquitectes.es
Pedra Tosca Park

Rosa Grena Kliass Arquitetura Paisagística
Rua Jesuíno de Arruda 888/131
04532-082 São Paulo, Brazil
Tel.: + 55 11 3167 4676
Fax: + 55 11 3167 4684
Parque da Juventude

Rush & Wright Associates
105 Queen Street, level 4
3000 Melbourne, Australia
Tel.: + 61 03 9600 4255
Fax: + 61 03 9600 4266
www.rushwirght.com
Grand Plaza
The Centre for Ideas

Santa-Rita Arquitectos
Rua Cidade de Nova Lisboa, Quinta da Fonte do Anjo
1800-107 Lisboa, Portugal
Tel.: + 35 218 53 80 58
Fax: + 35 218 53 80 60
City Park of Beja

Scapelab
Levstikov trg. 4°
1000 Ljubljana, Slovenia
Tel.: + 38 641 805 521
Fax: + 38 612 223 598
www.scapelab.com
Renovation of Čufarjev Square

SLA
Refshalevej A 153
DK-1432 Copenhagen, Denmark
Tel.: + 45 33 91 13 16
www.sla.dk
Charlotte Garden

SMC Alsop
41 Parkgate Road
SW11 4NP London, United Kingdom
Tel.: + 44 0 207 978 7878
Fax: + 44 0 207 978 7879
www.smcalsop.com
Clarke Quay Redevelopment

Stoa Architecture
27 rue Vacon
13001 Marseille, France
Tel.: + 33 04 91 33 16 71
Fax: + 33 04 91 54 78 97
www.stoa-architecture.com
Remodeling of Rauba Capeu

Studio Lazzaretto
Via San Senatire 2
20122 Milano, Italy
Tel.: + 39 02 72 09 40 34
Fax: + 39 02 72 09 40 34
Vittorio Veneto Square

Taylor Cullity Lethlean
385 Drummond Street
3053 Carlton, Victoria, Australia
Tel.: + 61 03 9380 4344
Fax: + 61 03 9348 1232
www.tcl.net.au
Forest Gallery

Todd Saunders/Saunders Architecture
Vestre Torggate 22
5015 Bergen, Norway
Tel.: + 47 55 36 85 06
Fax: + 47 97 52 57 61
www.saunders.no
Aurland Viewpoint

Tommie Wilhelmsen/Sivilarkitekt MNAL
Grannestunet 12
4052 Røyneberg, Norway
Tel.: + 47 91 74 44 76
www.tommie-wilhelmsen.no
Aurland Viewpoint

Toyo Ito & Architects Associates
Fujiya Bldg. 19-4, 1-Chome
150-0002 Shibuya, Shibuya-ku, Tokyo, Japan
Tel.: + 81 3 3409 5822
Fax: + 81 3 3409 5969
www.toyo-ito.com
Fira Montjuïc 2 in Barcelona

Turenscape
ZhongguanCun FaZhan DaSha, 12 ShangDi Xinxi Lu
100085 HaiDian District, Beijing, China
Tel.: + 86 1 062 967 408
Fax: + 86 1 062 988 905
www.turenscape.com
Dujiangyan Square
Zhongshan Shipyard Park

Urbanus Architecture & Design
Building E6, 2nd floor, OCT Loft
51 8053 Nashan District, Shenzhen, China
Tel.: + 86 755 860 963 45
Fax: + 86 755 861 063 36
www.urbanus.com.cn
Diwang Park B
Sungang Central Plaza

Verzone Woods Architectes
La Cure
CH-1659 Rougemont, Switzerland
Tel.: + 41 26 925 94 92
Fax: + 41 26 925 00 60
Las Margas Parks and Gardens

Vetsch Nipkow Partner Landschaftsarchitekten
Neumarkt 28
8001 Zurich, Switzerland
Tel.: + 41 43 244 82 00
Fax: + 41 43 244 82 10
www.vnp.ch
Katharina Sulzer Platz

Vladimir Djurovic Landscape Architecture
Rizk Plaza
Broumana, Lebanon
Tel.: + 961 4 862 444
Fax: + 961 4 862 462
www.vladimirdjurovic.com
Square Four Garden

West 8
Schiehaven 13 M
PO Box 6230
3002 AE Rotterdam, The Netherlands
Tel.: + 31 0 10 485 58 01
Fax: + 31 0 10 485 63 23
www.west8.nl
One North Park

Zade & Vilà Associats
Medes 4-6, 5° 1ª
08023 Barcelona, Spain
Tel.: + 34 93 210 35 62
Fax: + 34 93 210 35 62
Bosque de la vida